Ignatius of Loyola's Second Rules for Discernment

Ignatius of Loyola's Second Rules for Discernment

A User's Guide for Spiritual Directors

TIMOTHY M. GALLAGHER, OMV

A Crossroad Book
The Crossroad Publishing Company
New York

The Crossroad Publishing Company
www.CrossroadPublishing.com

Book design by Tim Holtz
Cover design by George Foster

ISBN: 9780824589035

Library of Congress Cataloging-in-Publication Data

Names: Gallagher, Timothy M., author.
Title: Ignatius of Loyola's Second rules for discernment : a user's guide for spiritual directors / Timothy M. Gallagher, OMV.
Description: New York : The Crossroad Publishing Company, [2023] | "A Crossroad book." | Includes bibliographical references. | Summary: "Ignatius's First Rules assist directors and their directees in discernments involving spiritual consolation and spiritual desolation. These fourteen rules provide invaluable aid at such times. Forty years of writing about, teaching, and applying these rules have shown me that Ignatius's First Rules are uniquely helpful when people struggle with spiritual desolation. These rules clarify the enemy's tactic and pointthe way to freedom. Our focus in this book, however, is Ignatius's Second Rules. In these eight rules, Ignatius addresses a more complex discernment. When a person has matured in the spiritual life, a time may come when the enemy changes tactics. Now he seeks less to discourage through spiritual desolation and begins, rather, to imitate the good spirit. He brings consolation with good, even holy thoughts-but directed toward a thing that God does not desire for this person. The enemy, Ignatius says, tempts this dedicated person under the appearance of good. If the temptation is not discerned, it will lead ultimately to harm for this person and for the others, usually many, whose lives this person touches. In his Second Rules, Ignatius provides a key to resolve such discernments"— Provided by publisher.
Identifiers: LCCN 2023049583 (print) | LCCN 2023049584 (ebook) | ISBN 9780824589035 (trade paperback) | ISBN 9780824598204 (epub)
Subjects: LCSH: Discernment of spirits. | Spiritual direction—Catholic Church—Handbooks, manuals, etc. | Ignatius, of Loyola, Saint, 1491-1556. Regulae ad spiritus dignoscendos.
Classification: LCC BV5083 .G34 2024 (print) | LCC BV5083 (ebook) | DDC 253.5/3—dc23/eng/20231207
LC record available at https://lccn.loc.gov/2023049583
LC ebook record available at https://lccn.loc.gov/2023049584

Books published by The Crossroad Publishing Company may be purchased at special quantity discount rates for classes and institutional use. For information, please email sales@CrossroadPublishing.com.

Contents

Acknowledgments

I am grateful to Gwendolin Herder of Crossroad Publishing for supporting this book from its beginning and making it possible; to Emily Wichland for her dedicated and competent assistance in the process of publication; to Harvey Egan, SJ, for his wise comments on the manuscript; to Lisa Gross and Adrienne Novatny for their reading of the text and their insights; and to Elizabeth Valeri for her attentive reading and invaluable assistance in the various stages of publication. To all, my sincerest thanks.

Introduction

Discernment is central to the spiritual life and so to spiritual direction. We, as directors, are privileged to accompany discerners through the process that leads to decision. A privilege, yes, and also a responsibility.

To assist us in this service, St. Ignatius of Loyola crafted two sets of rules for the discernment of spirits. In this book, I term these "First Rules" and "Second Rules."[1]

Ignatius's First Rules assist directors and their directees in discernments involving spiritual consolation and spiritual desolation.[2] These fourteen rules provide invaluable aid at such times. Forty years of writing about, teaching, and applying these rules have shown me that Ignatius's First Rules are uniquely helpful when people struggle with spiritual desolation. These rules clarify the enemy's tactic and point the way to freedom.

Our focus in this book, however, is Ignatius's Second Rules. In these eight rules, Ignatius addresses a more complex discernment. When a person has matured in the spiritual life, a time may come when the enemy changes tactics. Now he seeks less to discourage through spiritual desolation and begins, rather, to imitate the good spirit. He brings consolation with good, even holy thoughts—but directed toward a thing that God does not desire for this person. The enemy, Ignatius says, tempts this dedicated person *under the appearance of good.* If the temptation is not discerned, it will lead ultimately to harm for this person and for the others, usually many, whose lives this person touches. In his Second Rules, Ignatius provides a key to resolve such discernments.

When, as directors, we assist dedicated persons in this refined discernment, we turn to Ignatius's Second Rules. To apply them fruitfully, we need to understand them well, not only abstractly but also in practice. In this book, I seek to contribute to that practical understanding.

I write for spiritual directors. This book presumes the training, knowledge, and experience requisite for spiritual direction. It also presumes knowledge and experience of the First Rules. Familiarity with the Second Rules will assist the reader, but this book may also be read as an introduction to these rules.

It is intended to serve both those who offer spiritual direction and those learning to be spiritual directors. To the first, it provides a review and firmer grasp of the Second Rules in practice; to the second, a foundation on which experience will build.

This book is short. It seeks clarity in an area where clarity is often elusive. Its focus is the concrete application of the Second Rules in spiritual direction. In writing this book, therefore, I have not repeated the discussion of interpretations that I have treated elsewhere.[3]

Because the discernment treated in the Second Rules is refined, interpretations of them differ.[4] In this book, I follow the interpretation that I believe best understands these rules. This interpretation considers both Ignatius's text, the words he uses in these rules, and their context. Ignatius establishes this context in annotations 8–10 in the *Spiritual Exercises*. In the prologue to this book, I discuss it, and throughout the book present the Second Rules in its light.[5]

In this book, the eight rules are illustrated through an example. "Kathy," a spiritually mature person, faces the situation Ignatius envisages in his Second Rules. She must discern between her present fruitful service as a teacher and a call to more direct service to the poor. You are her director. You accompany her, and you help her apply the Second Rules. In the eight chapters of this book, we will explore how each of the eight rules may apply to Kathy's discernment.

Ignatius tells us that his Second Rules treat a "greater discernment of spirits" than the First Rules (*SpirEx*, 328). May this book assist spiritual directors when their directees face such discernment.

Text of the Second Rules*

Rules for the same effect with greater discernment of spirits, and they help more for the Second Week. (328)

First Rule. The first: it is proper to God and to his angels, in their movements, to give true joy and spiritual gladness, taking away all sadness and disturbance that the enemy induces; to whom it is proper to militate against that joy and spiritual consolation, bringing apparent reasons, subtleties, and persistent fallacies. (329)

Second Rule. The second: it is of God our Lord alone to give consolation to the soul without preceding cause; because it is proper to the Creator to enter, go out, to move it interiorly, drawing it totally in love of his divine majesty. I say without cause, without any previous sentiment or knowledge of some object, through which such a consolation comes, by means of its acts of understanding and will. (330)

Third Rule. The third: with cause both the good angel and the bad can console the soul, for contrary ends: the good angel for the profit of the soul, that it may grow and rise from good to better; and the bad angel for the contrary, and later on to draw it to his damnable intention and malice. (331)

Fourth Rule. The fourth: it is proper to the bad angel, who takes on the appearance of an angel of light, to enter with the devout soul and to go

* For this translation, see Gallagher, *Spiritual Consolation*, 7–9. In translating, I have sought closeness to Ignatius's original Spanish rather than literary elegance. The numbers in parentheses indicate the paragraph of the *Spiritual Exercises* where the text is found.

out with himself; that is, to bring good and holy thoughts, conformed to such a just soul, and afterward, little by little, he endeavors to go out, bringing the soul to his hidden deceits and perverse intentions. (332)

Fifth Rule. The fifth: we should give much attention to the course of the thoughts; and if the beginning, middle, and end is all good, inclined to all good, it is a sign of the good angel; but if in the course of the thoughts that he brings, it ends in something bad, or distractive, or less good than the soul had proposed to do before; or if it weakens it, or disquiets or troubles the soul, taking away the peace, tranquility, and quiet, which it had before, it is a clear sign that it proceeds from the bad spirit, the enemy of our profit and eternal salvation. (333)

Sixth Rule. The sixth: when the enemy of human nature has been perceived and known by his serpent's tail and the bad end to which he induces, it profits the person who was tempted by him to look immediately at the course of the good thoughts that he brought and the beginning of them, and how little by little he procured to make him descend from the sweetness and spiritual gladness in which he was, till he brought him to his depraved intention; so that with such an experience known and noted he may guard himself in the future from his customary deceits. (334)

Seventh Rule. The seventh: in those who proceed from good to better, the good angel touches such a soul sweetly, lightly and gently, as a drop of water that enters a sponge; and the bad touches it sharply and with noise and disquiet, as when the drop of water falls on a stone; and in those who proceed from bad to worse, the above-said spirits touch in a contrary way; the cause of which is that the disposition of the soul is contrary or similar to the said angels; for when it is contrary, they enter with clamor and sensible disturbances, perceptibly; and when it is similar, they enter with silence, as in their own house through an open door. (335)

Eighth Rule. The eighth: when the consolation is without cause, although there is no deception in it, since it is of God our Lord alone, as has been said, nevertheless the spiritual person to whom God gives such a consolation should, with much vigilance and attention, look at and distinguish the time itself of such an actual consolation from the time following, in which the soul remains warm and favored with the favor and remnants of the past consolation; for frequently, in this second time, through his own reasoning by associating and drawing consequences from ideas and judgments, or through the good spirit, or through the bad, he forms different proposals and opinions that are not given immediately by God our Lord, and therefore they must be very well examined before entire credit is given them or they are put into effect. (336)

Prologue

You are waiting for your next meeting of spiritual direction, and the doorbell rings. You answer and greet Kathy. You have accompanied her spiritually for six years and know her well. When you and Kathy are seated in your office, you pray briefly and prepare to listen.

Kathy is forty-five, a married woman with three children ages fifteen, fourteen, and twelve. She is a mature Christian with a faithful life of prayer and service in her family, work, and parish. Kathy is an accomplished high school teacher, appreciated by her students.

Her relationship with Jesus is the heart of her life, and you have seen this grow in recent years especially. Kathy's marriage has correspondingly deepened, and her presence creates a warm and loving center in the home.

Five years ago, the principal of the local Catholic high school approached Kathy and asked that she consider teaching in this school. He had been appointed principal a year earlier, commissioned with resolving the school's problems. For decades, the school had served the diocese well and was highly esteemed. It drew many students, and their families appreciated the solid education offered to their children. Graduation from this school guaranteed entrance into good colleges, and many former students held positions of responsibility in society.

More recently, however, things had changed. Poor management led to straitened finances and divisions among the faculty. As tensions increased, many of the staff, among them the best teachers, resigned. The quality of teaching declined, and parents looked elsewhere for their children. The school continued to deteriorate, and its survival was now in question.

Knowing Kathy's deep faith and professional competence, the principal asked her to consider a position at the school. He saw Kathy as a teacher who would enhance the academic level of the school, strengthen its Catholic dimension, foster unity, and might be key to its survival. Kathy sought your help to discern this request, and, after a well-made discernment, accepted the principal's offer.

She put her heart into teaching and helping the students. As the principal had foreseen, her presence and way of life strengthened the school's Catholic identity. Over the next five years, the school progressed well. Unity was restored, the quality of teaching improved, finances began to stabilize, and enrollment gradually increased. The school was moving toward viability. Kathy's warm, competent, and faith-filled presence contributed significantly to this growth. Well aware of this, the principal expressed his gratitude to Kathy. In your meetings with her, you have seen her grow spiritually through this service.

Now, Kathy begins to speak. She tells you that three weeks ago, as the fall semester began, she attended a meeting at a Catholic inner-city high school that serves disadvantaged students. Kathy was struck by the poverty of the surroundings and of the school itself. The needs of the students, the limited resources of the school, and the dedication of the staff deeply impressed her. Speaking over lunch with one of the faculty, she learned of the school's need for qualified teachers and the difficulty in finding them. The challenging conditions and modest salary deterred most candidates.

Kathy then shares an experience in prayer two weeks earlier. The Gospel text was Luke 4, and verse 18 especially spoke to her heart: "The Spirit of the Lord is upon me, because he has anointed me to preach good news to the poor."[6] The time of prayer was warm and suffused with awareness of God's closeness and love. As she pondered Jesus's predilection for the poor, the thought of the inner-city school returned. Might God be inviting her to share, in this way, more directly in Jesus's love for and mission to the poor? Might he be calling her to teach in this school? Joy accompanied this prospect. Her heart lifted at the thought of serving these impoverished students, of the new closeness with Jesus this might foster and the deeper self-giving this would permit. As she prayed, Kathy was moved to tears—blessed tears that expressed the joy her heart felt.

Kathy tells you that in her prayer, this thought and this joy have returned several times since. She wonders: Do the joy, the sense of God's love, and the desire for new closeness with Jesus that accompany the thought of the inner-city school indicate that God is asking her to teach there? Is this his way of revealing his call? When she has shared these experiences, Kathy ceases to speak and looks to you for help.

What will you say? What counsel will you offer? How will you help her?

Kathy is generous, a woman of faith and prayer, a mature disciple of Jesus. Her one desire is to heed God's call and do his will. She is ready, if God desires, to leave the upscale school and transfer to the inner-city school, thereby sharing more fully in Jesus's mission to the poor. Joy, warmth, and a sense of God's love for her and his closeness consistently accompany these thoughts.

In Ignatian terms, Kathy experiences spiritual consolation (First Rules, 3) when she contemplates teaching in the inner-city school. Ignatius writes that "in spiritual consolation the good spirit guides and counsels us more" (First Rules, 5). This spiritual consolation arises not once but various times when, in prayer, Kathy considers teaching in the inner-city school. A mature Christian, spiritual consolation, the recurrence of this consolation, a good and holy service, like Jesus, to the poor—is, then, the issue settled?

The question Kathy faces—and you as you accompany her—is this: Is the thought of the inner-city school and the spiritual consolation that accompanies it from the good spirit and a genuine call from God, a step that will lead to more fruitful service and bless Kathy herself? Or might it be a temptation from the enemy whose purpose is to undermine the growth of the upscale school and ultimately weaken Kathy as well?

The answer matters. Many will be affected by Kathy's decision either to remain in her present school or to move to the inner-city school. It also matters for Kathy's spiritual growth or diminishment.

In this situation, Ignatius's First Rules for discernment (*SpirEx*, 313–327) will not help. These fourteen rules assist a person to overcome spiritual desolation and its associated temptations. In the experience Kathy shares with you, spiritual desolation is not present. If the spiritual consolation she feels when she considers the inner-city school does not answer the question, then we must look beyond Ignatius's First Rules for guidance.

Kathy's experience is neither isolated nor rare. A pastor of a parish, for example, does fruitful work among his people. He begins to feel an attraction toward monastic life in order to grow in prayer, love God more deeply, and serve God's people through the contemplative life. The thought is accompanied by warm spiritual consolation. As time passes, the experience recurs. Is this a genuine call from God or a temptation of the enemy to undo his good work in the parish and subsequently harm the priest himself? The reverse may be said of the dedicated monk or contemplative sister who feels spiritual consolation at the thought of serving God actively outside the monastery.

A faith-filled woman with musical talent has led the parish choir for three years. The beauty of the music contributes to prayerful Masses, and Sunday attendance is rising. She notes the lack of young members in the choir and in the parish more generally. One day, she prays with Matthew 19:14, "Let the children come to me," and she begins to wonder if God is calling her also to work with the young of the parish. The thought is accompanied by warm spiritual consolation. A call from God? A temptation to divide her energies and weaken her present service?

A deacon with financial skills helps a parish to overcome its debt. Repairs urgently needed are now possible, and new life arises in the parish. As it does, the thought of an expanded role in the liturgy attracts him and awakens joy. The same questions apply.

A dedicated housewife offers valued help to a neighbor; a layman who loves the Lord guides a fruitful prayer group in his parish; a priest leads blessed retreat experiences for his parishioners; a Catholic speaker assists many with a rich message; a sister serves local immigrants with great love; a spiritual director accompanies his directees with warmth and wisdom.... In each case, he or she is spiritually consoled at the thought of an increased or different service. Is this of God and the next step in growth? Or is it a temptation that, if followed, will lead finally to diminishment?

In these cases, as in Kathy's, the person's discernment will affect not only the person him- or herself but many others as well. And, again, because spiritual desolation is not present, Ignatius's fourteen First Rules will not help resolve the discernment.

IGNATIUS PROVIDES AN ANSWER to these questions in his eight Second Rules. To understand them, however, we must examine three of his twenty annotations—that is, guidelines for one who gives the Spiritual Exercises (*SpirEx*, 1–20). In these three—annotations 8, 9, and 10—he clarifies when these eight rules apply.[7]

Annotation 8: Two Sets of Rules

Ignatius writes,

> The eighth: the one who gives the Exercises, according to the need he perceives in the one who receives them, with regard to the desolations and deceits of the enemy, and also with regard to the consolations, may explain to him the rules of the first and second weeks, which are for recognizing different spirits: para. 313 and 328.

Ignatius asks directors to note if the person is troubled by the spiritual desolations and deceits of the enemy, and to note the spiritual consolations as well. According to which tactic the enemy adopts with the person, the director should explain the first or the second set of rules. If the enemy employs a first strategy ("the desolations and deceits of the enemy"), the director will help this person by applying Ignatius's fourteen First Rules. If the enemy employs a second strategy ("spiritual consolations as well"), the director will help the person by applying Ignatius's eight Second Rules. The director, therefore, must know these two strategies of the enemy, recognize which the enemy employs with the person, and assist the person through the corresponding set of rules.

What, then, are these two strategies of the enemy and with whom does the enemy use the one or the other? Ignatius answers these questions in the two annotations that follow.

Annotation 9: The Enemy's First Strategy and Ignatius's First Rules

Ignatius explains,

> The ninth: it must be noted that, when the person who is making the Exercises is in the exercises of the First Week, if he is a person who has not been versed in spiritual things, and if he is tempted grossly and openly, such as showing him obstacles to going forward in the service of God our Lord, such as labors, shame, and fear for the honor of the world, etc.; the one who gives the exercises should not speak to him about the rules for different spirits of the Second Week; because as much as those of the First Week will help him, those of the Second Week will harm him, because this matter is too subtle and too elevated for him to understand.

The persons Ignatius intends have "not been versed in spiritual things." These are persons of faith who sincerely strive to live the spiritual life but have as yet limited understanding and experience of it. In terms of the Spiritual Exercises, these are persons "in the exercises of the First Week." A review of those exercises (*SpirEx*, 45–72) completes the profile of these persons: they are aware of their sin and actively seek purification from it; are conscious of what Christ suffered to free them from sin and so turn to him on the Cross, asking how they may better follow him; are grateful for God's mercy to them; seek freedom from what is disordered in their lives; and through contemplation of eternal loss, are strengthened in this resolve.

The enemy, Ignatius says, tempts these "grossly" (the temptations are unrefined, weighty, including baser levels) and "openly" (the temptations are evident, not hidden, clearly perceptible as temptations). Examples of such manifest temptations, Ignatius writes, include obstacles to progressing in the spiritual life: "It's so hard, costs so much effort, is so difficult to sustain. People will laugh at you, your friends will leave you, scorn you, lose respect for you. . . . Give it up, go back to the easier life you had before." The struggle will not be to identify such temptations as temptations—this will be clear to both directee and director—but to resist them.

Further, as the preceding annotation and Ignatius's First Rules abundantly indicate, such temptations will often be accompanied by spiritual desolation.[8] The enemy seeks to harm the "unversed" persons "of the First Week" through manifest (but potentially difficult to overcome) temptations and the discouragement of spiritual desolation.

I will speak of these persons as persons in the *first spiritual situation*: persons of faith, sincere in their love and service of God but who are still in the earlier stages of the spiritual life, still susceptible to the enemy's manifest temptations and the discouragement of spiritual desolation—the strategy, therefore, that the enemy employs with them.

For persons in this first spiritual situation—and this will be many of us—Ignatius's fourteen First Rules will be of great help. Directors who share these rules with such persons do them an enormous service: they equip their directees to notice, identify, and reject the enemy's spiritual desolations with their associated temptations.

In annotation 9, Ignatius enjoins on directors *not* to mention his Second Rules to persons in this first spiritual situation. The content of the Second Rules, he says, is "too subtle and too elevated" for them to understand. To speak of the Second Rules to those in the first spiritual situation will simply confuse them. Not only do they not need the Second Rules—because the enemy is not using the further strategy they envision—but the clarity of the First Rules that they very much need and are applying will be undermined.

To help their directees discern, therefore, directors will ask themselves, "Is he, is she, a person in the first or second spiritual situation?" In accordance with these persons' spiritual situations, directors will invite them to apply either Ignatius's First Rules or his Second Rules. Identifying whether directees are in the first or second spiritual situation "is one of the most important acts of the one who gives the Spiritual Exercises."[9] The same is true of spiritual direction in daily life outside the Spiritual Exercises.

What, then, is the second spiritual situation and how does it differ from the first spiritual situation? Ignatius turns to this question in the next annotation.

Annotation 10: The Enemy's Second Strategy and Ignatius's Second Rules

Ignatius writes,

> The tenth: when the one who gives the exercises perceives that the one who receives them is assaulted and tempted under the appearance of good, then it is proper to explain to him the rules for the Second Week already mentioned. For the enemy of human nature commonly tempts more under the appearance of good when the person is exercising himself in the illuminative life, which corresponds to the exercises of the Second Week, and not so much in the purgative life, which corresponds to the exercises of the First Week.

Ignatius now addresses to a different group of persons. These persons are "in the illuminative life, which corresponds to the exercises of the Second Week." These persons have already experienced, in some significant measure, "the purgative life, which corresponds to the exercises of the First Week"—that is, they have experienced and moved beyond the first spiritual situation described in the preceding annotation.

In terms of the Spiritual Exercises, these are persons of the Second Week. A review of the exercises of the Second Week (*SpirEx*, 91–168) identifies the profile of such persons: they seek complete availability to God's will; they are ready, should God desire, to imitate Jesus in his poverty and humiliation; they wish to know Jesus intimately, to love him more, to follow him more closely; they seek freedom from the deceptions of the enemy, to know the true life Jesus brings, and to imitate him in living it; they ask for grace to choose what will serve for God's greater glory.

Persons with such desires and who live according to them have passed beyond the first spiritual situation to the second spiritual situation. They seek increased purification from sin, but there are no major struggles in this regard. They love Jesus deeply and greatly desire to imitate him, a desire that embraces Jesus's suffering should God so desire. They are eager to do God's will and to dedicate their lives to his service. They are mature Christians, rooted in prayer, living fruitful lives in the world and the Church.[10]

With persons in this second spiritual situation, Ignatius says, the enemy no longer seeks to harm them through spiritual desolation and obvious temptations. Though they may at times struggle with these, they are unlikely to succumb to them. The enemy, therefore, adopts a new strategy.

Such persons will be "assaulted and tempted under the appearance of good." When, Ignatius says, a person is in the second spiritual situation, the enemy "commonly tempts more under the appearance of good."

"Under the appearance of good": Now the enemy will bring these persons joy and energy (spiritual consolation) toward a good thing, even a holy thing—but not the thing God desires for them. If they are deceived and choose this good and holy thing, their choice will lead ultimately to harm for them and to the others affected by their choice. "Commonly": This will be the habitual tactic of the enemy with the generous persons of the second spiritual situation. Such persons are very likely to experience this tactic of the enemy.

Consequently, persons in the second spiritual situation need help to note, identify, and reject temptations of the enemy under the appearance of good. Here, as we have seen, the First Rules will be of no assistance. Ignatius crafted his eight Second Rules precisely for this purpose: to help persons in the second spiritual situation reject the enemy's temptations under the appearance of good.

We may return now, in light of these annotations, to Kathy and her spiritual experience. Is Kathy a person of the first or second spiritual situation? She is "a mature Christian with a faithful life of prayer and service in her family, work, and parish." Her relationship with Jesus "is the heart of her life," and you, as her director, have seen this grow over the years and recently all the more. She lives her vocation as wife and mother fully, and "her presence creates a warm and loving center in the home." Professionally, her "warm, competent, and faith-filled presence" contributes greatly to her school and its students.

The characteristic traits of the first spiritual situation—substantial struggle to overcome sin, fear of what others will say of her Christian life, and the like—do not appear in this description. Is, then, Kathy a person in the second spiritual situation? Directors will note that this may well be so. They will recognize, therefore, that Ignatius's Second Rules may apply to her—that she may be tempted under the appearance of good.

The thought of teaching in the inner-city school is accompanied by joy and a sense of God's closeness (spiritual consolation). The thought itself is good and holy: the desire to imitate Jesus more fully in his love for the poor. Is this of the good spirit? Is it the next step toward growth in a generous and progressing spiritual life? Will it lead her to new intimacy with Jesus? Will it increase the fruitfulness of her service in the Church and world?

Or is it the enemy tempting under the appearance of good? Is the good and holy thought of serving the poor in the inner-city school and the spiritual consolation that accompanies it brought by the enemy to undo the valuable work she is doing in her present school as it moves toward new viability with the promise of rich fruits? Will it lead ultimately to discouragement and spiritual weakening in Kathy herself? The same questions apply to the other examples given above: Are the thoughts of new good and holy things and the spiritual consolation that accompanies them of the good spirit or of the enemy tempting under the appearance of good?

The answers are not obvious, nor are they immediately clear. Ignatius's Second Rules will provide the clarity that such discerners and their directors need.

Ignatius introduces his Second Rules with a brief and densely packed title:

> Rules for the same effect with greater discernment of spirits, and they help more for the Second Week.

This title follows immediately upon the First Rules, a context that clarifies its content. It contains three key affirmations about the Second Rules: these are rules for the same effect as the First Rules; they provide a greater discernment of spirits than the First Rules; and they apply to "Second Week" persons, those we have called persons in the second spiritual situation.[11]

The Second Rules "are for the same effect" as the First Rules. The reference is to the title of the First Rules in which Ignatius tells us that discernment of spirits consists in *becoming aware* of the spiritual movements in our hearts and thoughts, working with these until we *understand* what in them is of the good spirit and what is of the enemy, and taking the appropriate action: *accepting* what is of the good spirit and *rejecting* what is of the enemy. When we apply the Second Rules, Ignatius says, we will proceed by the same three steps: becoming aware; understanding; and taking action—that is, accepting or rejecting.

The Second Rules contain a "greater discernment of spirits" than the First Rules. In the first spiritual situation, the good spirit and the enemy employ *contrary* tactics: the good spirit gives spiritual consolation to encourage and enlighten the person; the enemy brings spiritual desolation to discourage and weaken the person. In the second spiritual situation, the good spirit and the enemy employ *similar* tactics: the good spirit continues to give spiritual consolation and good and holy thoughts; the enemy, however, changes course and imitates the good spirit. He also brings spiritual consolation and good and holy thoughts—but a deceptive spiritual consolation with deceptive thoughts, which, if not discerned, will harm these persons and diminish their service of God. Obviously discernment between similar tactics is a "greater," more refined discernment than discernment between contrary tactics.

Finally, these rules "help more for the Second Week"—that is, for Second Week persons, the mature, dedicated, generous persons of the second spiritual situation. As we have said, Kathy and all who, like her, deeply love the Lord and are zealous in Christian service, may well be such persons.

IN THE ANNOTATIONS and in his title statement, Ignatius clarifies the issue of discernment addressed in the Second Rules. The eight rules that follow provide a path through this delicate discernment.

CHAPTER 1

The Tactics of the Good Spirit and the Enemy

RULE 1

In the first of his Second Week rules, Ignatius describes the tactics of the good spirit and the enemy in the second spiritual situation. Let us suppose, for example, that as Kathy teaches in the upscale school, she employs the fall and spring semesters in discerning the call to the inner-city school. She meets with you monthly through this time, seeking your help with the discernment. Kathy, and you as her director, will watch for the signs of the good spirit and enemy outlined in Second Rules, 1. Ignatius writes,

> First Rule. The first: it is proper to God and to his angels, in their movements, to give true joy and spiritual gladness, taking away all sadness and disturbance that the enemy induces; to whom it is proper to militate against that joy and spiritual consolation, bringing apparent reasons, subtleties, and persistent fallacies.

"God" and "his angels" will give Kathy "true joy and spiritual gladness"—that is, spiritual consolation that takes away "all sadness and disturbance that the enemy induces." As in the first spiritual situation and first set of rules, the good spirit gives spiritual consolation. Such spiritual joy and gladness as the days of the discernment unfold are signs of the good spirit.

The enemy "militates against"—that is, strives to negate, to undo—"that joy and spiritual consolation." In the first spiritual situation, the enemy attempted this through the discouragement of spiritual desolation. With the mature persons of the second spiritual situation, as noted, the enemy changes his approach. His *goal* remains the same: to militate against the encouragement, strength, light, and growth that God gives through spiritual consolation. His *tactic*, however, changes. Now he attempts to deceive these persons through "apparent reasons, subtleties, and persistent fallacies."

Let us suppose that the spiritual consolation and thought of the inner-city school are of the enemy tempting under the appearance of good. During Kathy's time of discernment, the enemy will employ this tactic. He will bring "apparent reasons": as she ponders the call to the inner-city school, Kathy may find that reasons for this call present themselves—reasons that seem valid but are only apparently so. Carefully reviewed, they reveal a false quality. Likewise, "subtleties": as the discernment proceeds, the director notes that Kathy's thinking presents a complex, elaborate, convoluted quality that confuses her and the discernment. Finally, "persistent fallacies": skewed thinking, truths mingled with error, lines of thought that lead to false conclusions. A sign of this last tactic is its persistent quality: the director may note that Kathy returns again and again to such thinking.

The "apparent reasons, subtleties, and persistent fallacies," as the words *apparent* and *subtleties* indicate, will not be clamorous and often will not be immediately obvious. They will likely be identified only with time, as the discernment progresses. With goodwill, without fault, and unaware of the deception, Kathy and others in the second spiritual situation may pursue these for a time as they discern. Their directors will need to accompany them with attention, noting whether such thinking emerges during the discernment. If so, they will help their directees to perceive this. Because these persons only desire God's will, once the deception is revealed, they will firmly reject it. Later in the rules, Ignatius will describe more amply the setting in which this tactic of the enemy may emerge.

In Second Rules, 1, Ignatius simply highlights the tactics of the good spirit and enemy in the second spiritual situation. Obviously, this is helpful. Equally obvious, Second Rules, 1, does not fully equip directors to help Kathy or others like her discern. In the rules that follow, Ignatius will provide the tools directors need. He begins by describing a kind of spiritual consolation that clarifies the discernment.

CHAPTER 2

A Consolation That Resolves the Discernment

RULE 2

The days pass, and you and Kathy continue to meet. You have encouraged her to pray daily with Scripture, and she does so faithfully. Most mornings, she spends about an hour in prayer. You have taught her the examen prayer, and she prays this each evening. At your suggestion, she keeps a journal in which she records her spiritual experience in general and specifically in regard to the inner-city school.

First Meeting

You listen as Kathy describes various aspects of her spiritual life. After some minutes, she turns to the inner-city school. She tells you that she continues to experience joy when she contemplates this possibility. She feels God's closeness and love as she does so.

Then she says, "Last week, I prayed with Luke 6:20–22, the Beatitudes. I never got past the first beatitude, "Blessed are you poor, for yours is the kingdom of God" (Lk 6:20). I thought about Jesus's special love for the poor and how the kingdom of God belongs to them. I found that I couldn't move past this verse. I felt a deep sense of the Lord's closeness and love for me as I prayed. It filled the whole hour. I spent the next two days praying with this verse, and that joy and love never diminished. In all that time, I felt drawn to the inner-city school."

You note this experience, and you see, as does Kathy, its relevance to her discernment. With Kathy, you reverence the spiritual consolation given in her prayer. Regarding the discernment itself, you do not see clearly, nor do you attempt to anticipate that clarity. You trust that this will come as the process continues. Your calm and attentive presence, your assurance to Kathy that she is proceeding well in the discernment and that God will give the clarity she seeks, reassure Kathy, and she leaves encouraged in her discernment.

Second Meeting

Kathy tells you of another experience of prayer. The text this time is Luke 9:58: "Jesus answered him, 'Foxes have dens and birds of the sky have nests, but the Son of Man has nowhere to rest his head.'"

Kathy says, "This morning, I prayed with this text about one who wants to follow Jesus and Jesus's words about himself in reply. Like the passage in Luke 6, when I read these words, I just wanted to stay there. I felt especially how ready he was to follow wherever the Father would send him, without attachments to places or things. That freedom really drew my heart. The prayer was warm, and I felt loved. The hour passed so quickly. I will return to this tomorrow. As I prayed, I continued to feel attracted to the inner-city school."

Once more, you perceive the relevance of this experience to Kathy's discernment. However, you do not as yet see clearly in the discernment. You reverence Kathy's experience, and you note its unfolding. You warmly encourage Kathy to continue in her prayer with Scripture, her examen, and her journaling.

Third Meeting

Kathy shares similar experiences in prayer, especially when praying with Luke 16:19–31, the parable of the rich man and Lazarus, and Luke 18:18–30, the man whom Jesus calls to give his possessions to the poor and follow him. When other texts portray Jesus's own poverty and his love for the poor, she experiences a similar spiritual consolation. The attraction to the inner-city school continues to accompany this prayer.[12]

Fourth Meeting

When Kathy arrives, you note immediately that she is deeply moved. She tells you that last Saturday afternoon she went to a local retreat house.

She goes there for a few hours when she can and loves the peace and quiet prayer the house affords her.

Once there, Kathy prayed for a time, and then, in midafternoon, went out walking. She enjoyed the silence, the freshness of the winter cold, the snow, and the trees that overhung the path. She walked, thinking of nothing in particular, simply absorbing her surroundings.

Kathy says, "Then something happened that I've never experienced before. I don't quite know how to describe it. One minute I was just walking through the woods and then suddenly my heart was totally filled with a sense of God's love. It was overwhelming to feel so deeply, deeply loved. I was completely happy—the happiest I think I've ever been. God was close to me, loving me in a way I've never felt before. I don't know how long this lasted: maybe ten minutes, maybe fifteen, maybe more. I was so caught up in it, there was such sweetness and joy in it, that I could only receive it. And while this was happening, I knew that God is calling me to the inner-city school. It was so clear that I couldn't doubt it. The joy of that experience is gentler now, but it has not left me."

Kathy turns to you and asks, "Can you tell me what happened? What was this? Am I right that my discernment is done, that God has given me all the clarity I need? I am completely open to you, and I'll follow your guidance. But in that experience, I couldn't doubt that God was calling me to the inner-city school." Then she asks, "Can you help me?"

How will you help Kathy? Obviously she has received a wonderful, powerful experience of spiritual consolation. What can we say of such experiences? What place do they have in a process of discernment? Kathy is convinced that her discernment is concluded. Is she right? Should you affirm her conviction? Or must more be done?

In Second Rules, 2, Ignatius addresses such experiences and their role in discernment. He writes,

> Second Rule. The second: it is of God our Lord alone to give consolation to the soul without preceding cause; because it is proper to

> the Creator to enter, go out, to move it interiorly, drawing it totally in love of his divine majesty. I say without cause, without any previous sentiment or knowledge of some object, through which such a consolation comes, by means of its acts of understanding and will.[13]

There is, Ignatius says, one kind of spiritual consolation that only God can give. When, therefore, directees experience it, they may be sure that it is of God and not of the enemy. Directors help them by confirming their experience as this kind of spiritual consolation and explaining its meaning. When such spiritual consolation is given, the question Ignatius addresses in his Second Rules—Is this spiritual consolation and the thoughts that accompany it of the good spirit or of the enemy tempting under the appearance of light?—is resolved: this kind of spiritual consolation and any clarity it brings to discernment is surely of God and may be unhesitatingly followed.

What, then, is this kind of spiritual consolation that "God our Lord alone" can give? It is, Ignatius tells us, consolation "without preceding cause."

What does Ignatius mean by "preceding cause"? He explains, "I say without cause, without any previous sentiment or knowledge of some object, through which such a consolation comes, by means of its [the soul's] acts of understanding and will." That is, if spiritual consolation arises because in the time immediately preceding it, directees have focused their minds and hearts on some spiritual object (a verse of Scripture, a truth of faith, an aspect of God's creation, a memory of God's love and fidelity in the past, and similar spiritual "objects"), and through their active focus on this object the spiritual consolation arises, then, Ignatius affirms, their experience of spiritual consolation has a preceding cause.

A woman, for example, undergoes a difficult time in her spiritual life. Then the following occurs:

> One evening during this time, my eyes fell on the words: "O the depth of the riches and wisdom of God! How unsearchable are

> his judgements and how inscrutable his ways!" [Rom 11:33]. In the depths of my soul I became aware of a steadfast peace. The world could rock and reel. Everything and everyone could fail me. I myself could be broken, could be a complete failure in the eyes of men but nothing could prevent me from loving God.[14]

This woman experiences spiritual consolation—that is, an uplifting movement of the heart ("a steadfast peace") on the spiritual level, on the level of faith.[15] We may ask: Is this spiritual consolation *with* or *without* a preceding cause? In the time immediately preceding the spiritual consolation, this woman does focus on a spiritual "object"—the encouraging teaching of Romans 11:33—and actively opens her mind and heart to this teaching. Because she does, she experiences spiritual consolation. Had she not read Romans 11:33 and had she not focused her mind and heart on it, the spiritual consolation would not have arisen as it did. This woman experiences spiritual consolation *with* preceding cause.

A young woman recounts the following:

> I was fourteen years and three months when something happened—something that I have always believed to be a grace but have never been able to explain clearly. I suddenly found myself withdrawn—at least partly—from earthly things and plunged into an excessive and inexplicable joy, as if I were immersed in love and infinite gladness. I was intensely conscious of my state and at the same time of the impossibility of reflecting on it at the moment, and the certainty that I was with God. When I resumed contact with the familiar life around me—it was in the morning and I was doing some very ordinary housework, polishing a floor to be exact—I had acquired a new knowledge of God. Theoretically I knew nothing more than before . . . but to me God had ceased from that moment to be a kind of abstract idea . . . Now he had become a living being whom I knew henceforth, not only because I had been told about him . . . but because I had mystically perceived him, touched him. This event decided my life. It dominated

> it. The very memory of it, accompanied I may say by the memory of all the graces that followed and have marked my path, supports my life, sustains it, consoles it, delights it. I return to it again and again to renew my fervor.[16]

This woman, too, experiences spiritual consolation—that is, an uplifting movement of the heart ("inexplicable joy . . . immersed in love and gladness") on the spiritual level, on the level of faith. Again, we may ask: Is this spiritual consolation *with* or *without* a preceding cause? In the time immediately preceding the spiritual consolation, this woman is not focused on any spiritual object; she is simply polishing a floor. The spiritual consolation arises "suddenly," and she is "plunged into an excessive and inexplicable joy" with "the certainty that I was with God." It is, therefore, spiritual consolation *without* a preceding cause, simply given by God. She is, as Ignatius says, drawn "totally in love of his divine majesty." This woman, and any director to whom she might narrate this experience, may be sure that this spiritual consolation is of God along with the light it brings. ("This event decided my life.") Her account reveals the abundant fruit of such spiritual consolation.

Spiritual consolation *without* preceding cause is surely of God. If Kathy and persons like her receive such consolation and, with it, clarity regarding a discernment they face, that discernment is certain and may be concluded. Their directors' responsibility—the importance of which is evident—is to confirm whether the spiritual consolation was truly without cause.[17]

AIDED BY SECOND RULES, 2, we may return to Kathy's meetings with you. In your first meeting, Kathy shares the following:

> Last week, I prayed with Luke 6:20–22, the Beatitudes. I never got past the first beatitude, "Blessed are you who are poor, for the kingdom of God is yours." I thought about Jesus's special love for the poor and how the kingdom of God belongs to them. I found that I couldn't move past this verse. I felt a deep sense of the Lord's

> closeness and love for me as I prayed. It filled the whole hour. I spent the next two days praying with this verse, and that joy and love never diminished. In all that time, I felt drawn to the inner-city school.

As you listen to Kathy, you recognize that she has received a rich experience of spiritual consolation. You also perceive that this is spiritual consolation *with* preceding cause. It is a blessed experience and significant for Kathy's discernment. It does not, however, of itself resolve the discernment. It is not the spiritual consolation without preceding cause that Ignatius says only God can give. Thus, you recognize that Second Rules, 2, does not apply. You reverence Kathy's experience of spiritual consolation but know that the discernment must continue.

The same is true of the spiritual consolation that Kathy shares in your second and third meetings. When she prays with Luke 9:58, 16:19–31, and 18:18–30, she experiences spiritual consolation with preceding cause.

The spiritual consolation Kathy describes in your fourth meeting is very different. She tells you that she was outdoors, thinking of nothing in particular, simply absorbing her surroundings:

> Something happened that I've never experienced before. I don't quite know how to describe it. One minute I was just walking through the woods, and then suddenly my heart was totally filled with a sense of God's love. It was overwhelming to feel so deeply, deeply loved. I was completely happy—the happiest I think I've ever been. God was close to me, loving me in a way I've never felt before. I don't know how long this lasted: maybe ten minutes, maybe fifteen, maybe more. I was so caught up in it, there was such sweetness and joy in it, that I could only receive it. And while this was happening, I knew that God is calling me to the inner-city school. It was so clear that I couldn't doubt it.

As you listen, you see the signs of spiritual consolation without preceding cause. Kathy is not focused on any spiritual object in the time immediately preceding the spiritual consolation.[18] The consolation is simply given, poured out upon her, and with an abundance that recalls Ignatius's "drawing it [the soul] totally in love of his divine majesty."

You perceive that, in all likelihood, God has given Kathy spiritual consolation without preceding cause and that, during this experience, she has received clarity regarding her discernment: God is calling her to the inner-city school. If this is indeed spiritual consolation without preceding cause, as every indication suggests, then Kathy's discernment is concluded. Your part is to explain to Kathy, in light of Second Rules, 2, what she has experienced and to confirm that her discernment is complete.

Two practical questions remain, and we will address them here.

How often does spiritual consolation without preceding cause occur?

The question is not abstract. Essentially it asks: How frequently may spiritual directors expect to encounter spiritual consolation without preceding cause in directees' experience?[19]

Ignatius does not address this question, and the commentators are divided. Some consider it common experience; others see it as rare and reserved to exceptionally holy people. My own best answer, after decades of spiritual direction, is that it does indeed occur in directees' experience, but not with great frequency. Spiritual directors should not expect to encounter such consolation regularly. Over their years of spiritual direction, they may recognize it on occasion. As is evident, they provide an important service to directees when they do.

What if a directee shares an experience that might be spiritual consolation without preceding cause but you are not sure?

One author's principle applies here: "In discerning, we use the material that is clear. We may let the rest go, and remain in peace."[20] A directee, for example, shares an experience and you help him or her describe it more fully. Neither the directee nor you, however, sees clearly whether this is spiritual consolation without preceding cause. In this case, with the directee you reverence the spiritual consolation received, you note it as part of the discernment, and as this author says, you encourage the directee to continue the discernment with peace—a peace that you also share as director.

This peace is important. If the enemy is tempting a person in the second spiritual situation under the appearance of good, most often the discernment will not be initially clear. When, as director, you experience this initial unclarity—in your first meetings, you do not see clearly whether God is calling Kathy to the inner-city school—you may be at peace and help your directees also to be at peace. If the means for discernment (prayer, examen, journaling, and the like) are used well, and if Ignatius's Second Rules are properly applied, the needed clarity will come.[21]

In dealing with initial unclarity and with spiritual consolation without preceding cause, competent supervision will greatly assist directors. If this is true generally, it is the more so in such refined matters of discernment.

CHAPTER 3

Consolation from the Good Spirit and the Enemy

RULE 3

When Kathy receives spiritual consolation without preceding cause, her discernment is complete: only God can give such consolation. With Ignatius, we turn now to the more common case in which consolation without preceding cause is *not* given. What do you do, then, as Kathy's spiritual director? When she feels drawn to the inner-city school, her attraction and the joy that accompanies it may be of the good spirit or of the enemy tempting under the appearance of good. How do you help her or any other dedicated person in like circumstances?

This is the question you will most often face when applying the Second Rules. Ignatius turns to it now.

To EXEMPLIFY THIS QUESTION, we will return to the first three meetings with Kathy as given in the preceding chapter. We will also assume that her experience of spiritual consolation without preceding cause did not take place.

In that first meeting, Kathy tells you that she experiences spiritual consolation when she considers teaching in the inner-city school. She describes praying with Luke 6:20–22 and says, "I felt a deep sense of the Lord's closeness and love for me as I prayed. It filled the whole hour. I spent the next two days praying with this verse, and that joy and love never diminished. In all that time, I felt drawn to the inner-city school."

In the next meeting, Kathy recounts that when she prayed with Luke 9:58, "I just wanted to stay there. I felt especially how ready he was to follow wherever the Father would send him, without attachments to places or things. That freedom really drew my heart. The prayer was warm, and

I felt loved. The hour passed so quickly. I will return to this tomorrow. As I prayed, I continued to feel attracted to the inner-city school." In her prayer, Kathy continues to experience spiritual consolation with the same energy toward the inner-city school.

The pattern continues in the third meeting as Kathy relates the spiritual consolation she experienced when praying with Luke 16:19–31 and 18:18–30. Again, a desire for the inner-city school accompanies her times of prayer.

So . . . what is happening? How do you help Kathy discern this spiritual consolation and its accompanying attraction to the inner-city school? Is it of God? Not of God? You note that Kathy's experiences of consolation are experiences of spiritual consolation *with* preceding cause. You know, therefore, that Second Rules, 2, will not assist you here.

Ignatius dedicates Second Rules, 3–7, the majority of his rules, to addressing precisely this question: When generous persons in the second spiritual situation experience spiritual consolation with preceding cause and, as they do, a drawing toward some new service of God, how will they know whether this drawing is of the good spirit or the enemy?

IGNATIUS WRITES,

> Third Rule. The third: with cause both the good angel and the bad can console the soul, for contrary ends: the good angel for the profit of the soul, that it may grow and rise from good to better; and the bad angel for the contrary, and later on to draw it to his damnable intention and malice.

Ignatius's first words alert directors to a key truth: "*With cause* both the *good angel* and *the bad* can console the soul." Kathy, as she prays—or any person in the second spiritual situation—receives spiritual consolation *with* preceding cause: this kind of consolation may be given *both* by the good angel and the bad.

In the second spiritual situation, the enemy imitates the good spirit and brings spiritual consolation with preceding cause. Only God can give spiritual consolation *without* preceding cause (Second Rules, 2); both the good spirit and the enemy can give spiritual consolation *with* preceding cause (Second Rules, 3).

With this teaching in mind, you note that Kathy's experiences of spiritual consolation with accompanying drawing to the inner-city school are experiences of spiritual consolation *with* preceding cause. These consolations arise as she prays with Gospel texts and opens her mind and heart to them. Thus, the fact that she experiences such consolations does not resolve the discernment. These spiritual consolations with the attraction to the inner-city school may be of the good spirit and a sign that God is calling her to this school, but they may also be of the enemy and therefore deceptive.

Both spirits may adopt a similar tactic—spiritual consolation with preceding cause and a drawing to a good thing—but they do so for contrary purposes. The good spirit does this "for the profit of the soul, that it may grow and rise from good to better." If her consolations and her desire for the inner-city school are of the good spirit, in pursuing this call Kathy will grow and her service will become more fruitful. The enemy adopts this tactic, however, "for the contrary, and later on to draw it [the soul] to his damnable intention and malice." If Kathy's consolations and her desire for the inner-city school are of the enemy, in pursuing this call Kathy will experience spiritual harm and her service will become less fruitful.

Second Rules, 3, is highly important for spiritual directors. It tells them that with generous persons in the second spiritual situation, spiritual consolation of itself will most often not resolve the discernment. This will be true only of spiritual consolation *without* preceding cause. In the more common case of spiritual consolation *with* preceding cause, the consolation and its accompanying thoughts must be discerned well.

How will that discernment be reached? In Second Rules, 3, Ignatius simply states the issue. To see this clearly in Kathy's case or any like it is, however, a great service to directors. It protects them from assuming that when generous people receive spiritual consolation, it must always be of God and that the thoughts that accompany it are necessarily of God and to be followed. It tells them that discernment is needed first.

Second Rules, 3, offers a first brief allusion to how such discernment may be attained. The enemy, Ignatius says, gives consolation with preceding cause in order to draw the person "later on" to the harm he intends. Careful attention to this "later on" will supply the needed clarity. In his next rule, Ignatius turns to this.

CHAPTER 4

The Enemy's Tactic Described

RULE 4

Ignatius's Second Rules, 4, reads as follows:

> Fourth Rule. The fourth: It is proper to the bad angel, who takes on the appearance of an angel of light, to enter with the devout soul and to go out with himself; that is, to bring good and holy thoughts, conformed to such a just soul, and afterward, little by little, he endeavors to go out, bringing the soul to his hidden deceits and perverse intentions.

This rule, too, is of great importance for directors. In it, Ignatius outlines the tactic of the enemy when tempting generous persons under the appearance of good. Knowing his tactic, and with the further counsels given in the next three rules, directors will be equipped to help Kathy and anyone like her in their discernments.

The enemy, Ignatius says, when tempting generous persons under the appearance of good, "even Satan disguises himself as an angel of light" (2 Cor 11:14). He explains: it is "proper" to the enemy—that is, what follows describes how the enemy characteristically works when taking on the appearance of an angel of light—"to *enter* with the devout soul and to *go out* with himself."

The enemy, Ignatius says, when operating as an angel of light, enters "with the devout soul." That is, he begins (enters) by bringing spiritual consolation (with preceding cause) and holy thoughts, a consolation and holy thoughts that align well with the generous person of the second spiritual situation.

If, for example, the enemy is tempting Kathy under the appearance of good, he will begin by bringing her spiritual consolation (with preceding cause) and holy thoughts (increased communion with Jesus in his poverty and love for the poor by teaching in the inner-city school). He will enter "with the devout soul."

Generous persons like Kathy are unlikely to succumb to evident temptations. When the enemy tempts them, therefore, he takes on the appearance of an angel of light and imitates the good spirit, bringing these persons spiritual consolation (with preceding cause) and holy thoughts—holy thoughts of some good service that God does not desire for them.

He does this only to harm such persons. If he enters with the devout soul, it is only in order to "go out with himself"—that is, to lead these persons "later on" to succumb to his deceits.

Ignatius then amplifies his description of the enemy's tactic and articulates it according to three moments. The first is the *beginning* of his tactic—"that is, to bring good and holy thoughts, conformed to such a just soul." If, again, we presume for the moment that Kathy's attraction to the inner-city school is a temptation of the enemy, then this beginning occurs when Kathy prays with Jesus's words in the synagogue, as she related in her first meeting with you (chapter 2). The Gospel text was Luke 4, and verse 18 especially spoke to her heart: "The Spirit of the Lord is upon me, because he has anointed me to preach good news to the poor." The time of prayer was warm and suffused with awareness of God's closeness and love. As she pondered Jesus's predilection for the poor, the thought of the inner-city school returned. Might God be inviting her to share, in this way, more directly in Jesus's love for and mission to the poor? *Might he be calling her to teach in this school*? Joy accompanied this prospect. Her heart lifted at the thought of serving these impoverished students, of the new closeness with Jesus this might foster, and the deeper self-giving this would permit. As she prayed, Kathy was moved to blessed tears that expressed the joy her heart felt.

Kathy experiences warm spiritual consolation with preceding cause. As she does, "good and holy thoughts" arise: Might the Lord be calling her to new closeness with Jesus in his poverty and love for the poor through the inner-city school? Yes, good and holy thoughts of greater self-giving, greater service, deeper union with Jesus.

These thoughts are, Ignatius adds, "conformed to such a just soul." Presuming once more that these thoughts are of the enemy, it is evident that they are indeed "conformed" to the "just soul"—that is, to Kathy, the competent and dedicated teacher who loves her students and whose heart goes out to the poor. The enemy does not bring her thoughts, for example, of assisting the poor in the parish, serving as catechist, working with refugees, helping in retreats, evangelizing through media, and the like. He brings her thoughts *conformed* to her personal capabilities and heart. Because these thoughts are conformed to such generous persons, they are the more likely—unless discerning—to be deceived by them.

If these thoughts are of the enemy and Kathy is not discerning, they will lead to the enemy's intended *end*: "He endeavors to go out, bringing the soul to his hidden deceits and perverse intentions." In Kathy's case, this would mean deciding, with good intentions but unaware of the enemy's deception, to teach in the inner-city school when, in fact, this is not God's will for her. If she acts on this decision, unhappy consequences will follow. The growth of the upscale high school will be threatened, and Kathy may grow discouraged if she finds herself, for example, unable to cope well and teach fruitfully in the inner-city school. In these circumstances, her spiritual life is likely to suffer as well.

Ignatius speaks here of the enemy's "*hidden* deceits."[22] Another key point is touched here. Generous persons in the second spiritual situation only desire God's will and are ready to embrace it with wholehearted self-giving. If, in fact, the thoughts of the inner-city school are of the enemy, Kathy will only pursue them as long as the deceit is *hidden* from her, as long as she does not perceive that these thoughts are of the enemy. In the moment itself that she, with her director's help, grasps that these thoughts are of the enemy, she will reject them. In the second spiritual situation, for the enemy, to be seen is to be undone.

In the enemy's tactic, between the *beginning* and the *end* there is a *middle*, during which he endeavors "little by little" to lead the person to his desired end. "Little by little"—that is, by small gradual steps. Because this process occurs little by little, these generous persons are less likely to perceive it. In Kathy's case, this "little by little" will occur during the months of her discernment. This middle is the time when the enemy will bring the "apparent reasons, subtleties, and persistent fallacies" described in Second Rules, 1.

The enemy's astute tactic will also be his undoing if Ignatius's Second Rules are applied to the beginning, middle, and end of the discernment.

Directors will note Ignatius's focus on the good and holy *thoughts* the enemy brings to these generous persons. He will pursue this focus in the two following rules as well.

A fundamental element of discernment in the second spiritual situation is present here. Both the good spirit and the enemy can give spiritual consolation with preceding cause. Is there a difference in *quality* between the spiritual consolation given by the one spirit and the other? If there is, could this difference in quality be used to discern from which spirit the consolation comes?

Such a difference in quality may exist. If it does, however, discernment by this difference would be so difficult that Ignatius does not attempt it. Rather, he turns to something exterior to the spiritual consolation itself—that is, to the good and holy *thoughts* that arise with it. In order to discern, he asks us to note what happens in the person as these thoughts unfold little by little and reach their end.

For Kathy, this means that her director will help her discern not by examining the quality of the spiritual consolation—it is enough to know that it is spiritual consolation with preceding cause and that therefore both the good spirit and the enemy can give it—but by attending to her good and holy thoughts about the inner-city school and to what happens as these unfold during the discernment.

It also means that most often, when directees like Kathy first present experiences of spiritual consolation with preceding cause and good and holy thoughts of some new step in God's service, you will not see clearly whether this is of the good spirit or of the enemy tempting under the appearance of good. Such is the case when Kathy first tells you about her experience of praying with Luke 4:18 as recounted in the prologue.

Directors, therefore, in light of Ignatius's Second Rules, must not feel anxious or inadequate because they do not perceive clearly in the first meeting or in those that follow soon after whether the good spirit or the enemy is at work in these good and holy thoughts. They can be at peace, confident that if they apply the Second Rules well, clarity will emerge as the beginning becomes the middle and leads to the end. The directors' peace with this initial unclarity also helps their directees to pursue discernment without anxiety.

How, THEN, SHOULD DIRECTORS help Kathy or anyone like her facing such discernment? They help by recognizing that these are persons in the second spiritual situation; that they have received spiritual consolation with preceding cause and good and holy thought about some new step in God's service; that this consolation and these thoughts may be of the good spirit or of the enemy tempting under the appearance of good; that the discernment generally will not be immediately clear; that these persons and their directors should note this initial unclarity without anxiety; that these persons, aided by their directors, should apply Ignatius's Second Rules in this discernment; and that if they do, and both directors and directees fulfill their respective roles, the discernment will become clear.

As needed, directors will explain Ignatius's Second Rules to their directees. They will invite their directees to pray daily and to review the experience of their prayer (*SpirEx*, 77). They will explain the examen prayer to them and encourage them to pray it daily.[23] Journaling as they review their prayer and examine the day will benefit the discernment. Through journaling about it, they will grasp their experience more deeply, and their journal will help them express this experience more fully when they meet with their directors. Attention to spiritual experience, to consolations and their accompanying thoughts as these unfold, is the indispensable means for unmasking the enemy's temptations under the appearance of good. Regular meetings with their directors, perhaps more frequently than usual when discerning, will assist this attention and enlighten the process of discernment.

Directors will need to keep the Second Rules fresh in their awareness. Their key role is to help their directees attend to their spiritual experience and to note carefully what their directees share. This is the "much attention" (Second Rules, 5) and "much vigilance and attention" (Second Rules, 8) to which Ignatius calls them and their directees in Second Rules discernment. Attention to this experience, understood in light of the Second Rules, will lead to a sound discernment.

THE ENEMY'S TACTIC, Ignatius tells us, develops according to three successive moments:

BEGINNING

MIDDLE

END

In his next three rules, Ignatius equips directors to help directees discern in each of these three moments. The enemy can imitate the good spirit in the beginning of his tactic, bringing spiritual consolation with preceding cause and good and holy thoughts. However, because his end is contrary to that of the good spirit, the further the process unfolds toward that end, the more—to one who is attentive—the signs of his deceptions will appear.

Ignatius, in his treatment of these three moments, begins with the *end*, the time when the enemy's deceits are most evident (Second Rules, 5). He then addresses the *middle* (Second Rules, 6). Finally, he examines the *beginning* of the enemy's temptations and how discernment may be possible even then (Second Rules, 7).

CHAPTER 5

The Clearest Signs of the Enemy

RULE 5

Second Rules, 5, is "one of the most important among all the rules that Ignatius gives."[24] This rule supplies the clearest criteria for discerning whether, when a generous person receives spiritual consolation with preceding cause and good and holy thoughts, these are of the good spirit or of the enemy. Ignatius writes,

> Fifth Rule. The fifth: We should give much attention to the course of the thoughts; and if the beginning, middle, and end is all good, inclined to all good, it is a sign of the good angel; but if in the course of the thoughts that he brings, it ends in something bad, or distractive, or less good than the soul had proposed to do before; or if it weakens it, or disquiets, or troubles the soul, taking away the peace, tranquility, and quiet, which it had before, it is a clear sign that it proceeds from the bad spirit, the enemy of our profit and eternal salvation.

"We should give *much attention*": As we have said, this attentiveness is the primary task of directors and directees when discerning in the second spiritual situation. Ignatius, who never uses a superfluous adverb, calls both directors and directees to *much* attention. This attention, always important in discernment, is never more so than when discerning the enemy disguised as an angel of light.

To what should directors and directees be attentive? Ignatius writes, "We should give much attention *to the course of the thoughts*."[25] In the second spiritual situation, the enemy imitates the good spirit and brings "good and holy thoughts, conformed to such a just soul" (Second

Rules, 4). Kathy receives spiritual consolation with preceding cause and good and holy thoughts about teaching in the inner-city school. Is this of the good spirit? Is it of the enemy disguised as an angel of light? How will she know?

Ignatius calls us to attend to the *course* of these thoughts—that is, to their unfolding over the time of discernment. In her successive meetings with you, Kathy, for example, may share further thoughts about teaching in the inner-city school, additional reasons for this choice, new considerations regarding the transition, different thoughts about the timing of the move or how to prepare for it, and the like. You note that the thoughts about the inner-city school are unfolding as you and Kathy meet—you perceive that there is *a course of thoughts* regarding the inner-city school.

Ignatius calls directors and discerners to attend closely to this course of thoughts and to what happens in the discerners as it unfolds. Most discernments of the enemy disguised as an angel of light will be resolved through attention to this course of thoughts.

The enemy can imitate the good spirit well in the beginning of these thoughts. Like the good spirit, he can bring consolation and good and holy thoughts. But, to an attentive eye, his ability to deceive decreases as the thoughts unfold. As these enemy-inspired thoughts move progressively toward their end—a choice contrary to God's will for the person—the deception will be increasingly manifest—that is, manifest to directors and discerners who give much attention to the course of the thoughts and to its effect on the discerners.

Because the enemy seeks ultimately to distance the person from God's will, these thoughts, as they unfold over time, will cause a spiritual diminishment in the discerner. This diminishment will not be blatant—these are the generous persons of the second spiritual situation, who only want God's will—but it will be present. If director and discerner give much attention to the course of the thoughts, they will perceive it. Should they do so, they will know that this consolation and these thoughts are of the enemy.

WHAT, THEN, ARE THE SIGNS of this diminishment and that this course of thoughts is of the enemy? And what are the signs that it is *not* of the enemy but of the good spirit? Ignatius answers these questions in the remainder of Second Rules, 5. He gives first the signs of the good spirit and then those of the enemy.

"If," he tells us, "the beginning, middle, and end is all good, inclined to all good, it is a sign of the good angel." We will exemplify this in detail shortly, but for the moment let us apply this briefly to Kathy and the inner-city school. The beginning certainly is "all good, inclined to all good." Kathy experiences spiritual consolation and the thoughts that arise with it are clearly good: closer union with Jesus and greater sharing in his love for the poor through teaching in the inner-city school.

Kathy enters a process of discernment regarding this call. If not only the *beginning* (when she first prays with Luke 4:18) but also the *middle* (the months of discernment) and the *end* (Kathy discerns that God is calling her to the inner-city school) show *no sign* of spiritual diminishment—she continues to be spiritually alive, close to the Lord, faithful in prayer, generous in service, even increasingly so as she considers the inner-city school—then this course of thoughts "is all good, inclined to all good," and the signs of the good spirit are present.

But if the course of these thoughts "ends in something bad, or distractive, or less good than the soul had proposed to do before" (objective criteria); or "if it weakens it, or disquiets, or troubles the soul, taking away the peace, tranquility, and quiet, which it had before (affective criteria), "it is a clear sign that it proceeds from the bad spirit, the enemy of our profit and eternal salvation." If you note signs of such diminishment in Kathy as the course of the thoughts unfolds, then you know clearly that the consolation and the thoughts that accompanied it were of the enemy from the beginning.

Ignatius describes the signs of this diminishment: the course of the thoughts ends in something *bad* (for this person—Kathy, for example, will not adapt well to the inner-city school, does not have the health for it, and so forth), *distractive* (she will be taken from her valuable work in the upscale high school at a key time for its future), or *less good* (her service in the inner-city school will be valuable but be less so than her current role).

Ignatius adds a second set of affective signs of diminishment. If, as the course of the thoughts unfolds, it *weakens* Kathy (her spiritual energy declines, her prayer is less consistent and fervent, her courage in God's service diminishes), or it *disquiets* and *troubles* her (Kathy loses her former peace in the Lord, she is more troubled than before), then clear signs of the enemy are present.

In sum: Is there no diminishment, whether objective or affective, and is the course of the thoughts as it unfolds all good and inclined to all good? Then the thoughts are of the good spirit—God is calling Kathy to the inner-city school. Is there an objective or affective diminishment as the course of the thoughts unfolds? Then these thoughts are of the enemy and are to be rejected: God is not calling Kathy to the inner-city school.

It is to the presence or absence of such diminishment that both Kathy and you will give much attention as the months of the discernment pass. If you do so, the discernment will be clear.

A further reflection is important for directors. Ignatius provides means for discerning the middle (Second Rule, 6) and end (Second Rules, 5) of the course of thoughts. That he does so indicates his expectation that very often—most often, in fact—we will not discern the presence of the enemy in the beginning and early stages of the discernment. We need not be troubled, then, if we cannot discern clearly in these early stages.

Thus, when Kathy meets with you and tells you of her prayer with Luke 4:18, in all likelihood you will not know which spirit is at work. You may be at peace with this, and you can help Kathy to be at peace with this as well. Very likely, also, you will not see clearly in the next few meetings. Again, both you and Kathy can be at peace. What matters is to focus much attention to the course of the thoughts with an eye to the signs of the good spirit or the enemy. Such attention will lead to clarity.[26]

We will look now at two different directions in which your meetings with Kathy may develop. As we do, we will watch for the signs of the good spirit or the enemy.

In a first meeting, Kathy told you of her visit to the inner-city school and of her prayer two weeks later with Luke 4:18. She shared with you the warm consolation she experienced as she prayed with this verse and that the thought arose: Might God be calling me to teach in the inner-city school? Might this be a new step in closer union with Jesus and deeper sharing in his love for the poor? She added that she had experienced a similar consolation and thoughts about the inner-city school at other times since.

You listened warmly to her sharing. When she finished, you did not see clearly whether this was a call from the Lord. You recognized that Kathy is very likely a person in the second spiritual situation who might, therefore, be tempted by the enemy under the appearance of good. You noted that her spiritual consolation was consolation with preceding cause and that, consequently, it and the thoughts of the inner-city school that accompanied it could be of the good spirit but might also be of the enemy. You saw that light on this discernment would come not from Ignatius's First Rules but from his Second Rules.

You encouraged Kathy to continue to pray. You invited her to review her prayer as Ignatius counsels (*SpirEx*, 77) and to pray the daily examen. You suggested that she journal about any further experiences in this regard. Your warmth, your reverence for her sharing, and your calm instilled peace in Kathy. She left heartened and ready to follow your advice.

First Scenario

Second Meeting

Kathy returns to meet with you. She mentions some significant experiences in teaching during the past weeks and shares her spiritual experience during this time. As she speaks, Kathy again refers to the thought of the inner-city school. This thought continues to awaken joy and a sense of closeness with the Lord. When Kathy considers teaching in the inner-city school and so serving the poor like Jesus, she feels loved by God, and she is drawn to this choice. She tells you that she has no greater clarity than before, only that the attraction remains and it brings her joy in the Lord.

You listen attentively as she speaks and help her with opportune questions to describe her experience more fully. This time, too, you do not see clearly whether the thought of serving in the inner-city school is of God. You remain calm, and your calm gives Kathy peace. You affirm her daily fidelity to prayer, the review, the examen, and journaling, and you encourage her to continue with this. She leaves encouraged and prepared to continue the discernment.

You remain calm because you know that if both of you continue to be attentive, the signs of the good spirit or the enemy will emerge.

Third Meeting

Kathy speaks of her prayer and her teaching, both of which have been rewarding in the past weeks. Again she shares her joy at the thought of teaching in the inner-city school. This thought recurs from time to time, always with an uplift of heart.

You listen carefully to what Kathy shares but as yet you have no clarity regarding her discernment. You commend her fidelity to prayer and review, and you encourage her to continue with this.

Fourth Meeting

Kathy remains fulfilled in her teaching, essentially joyful, and her prayer is alive. The question of the inner-city school arises once more. Kathy tells you that she is proficient in Spanish and now wonders whether, were she to teach in an inner-city school, a school in which Spanish is needed might be best. A similar school would permit her to place this talent at the service of the disadvantaged.

Again, you do not see clearly in the discernment. You note the progression of the thoughts about the inner-city school. A new element has entered, that of Spanish and an inner-city school in which this language is needed. You listen warmly and affirm Kathy's faithful prayer and review. Once more, she leaves in peace.

Fifth Meeting

Kathy shares her spiritual experience of the preceding weeks, a time of occasional struggles but above all of joy in her teaching and at home, with consolation in prayer. She says that the thought of the inner-city school remains and continues to be a source of joy in the Lord. Kathy tells you that were she to seek a Hispanic inner-city school, the one in which she taught during graduate school might be the best. She was well received there, and she knows that the principal will need a new teacher in the coming year.

You note the further development of the thoughts: you perceive a course of thoughts unfolding. You do not yet see clearly in the discernment, and you recognize the need for "much attention" as this course of thoughts develops, watching for the signs of the good spirit or the enemy.

Sixth Meeting

Kathy tells you that a review of her present high school's buildings has concluded that renovations are necessary for the school's future. A new capital campaign would have to be undertaken, and the teachers would be involved. They would also have to teach in reduced quarters during the year of renovations that would follow the campaign. Kathy says that her heart sank a little when she thought of the time and energy this would require but that she was willing to do what the school needed. She adds that it would be easier to undertake this effort were it for the poor of an inner-city school where the need is so great rather than in a well-to-do suburban school. In general, her teaching has gone well, and her prayer has been consoled in the Lord.

You note that, for the first time, Kathy has expressed movements of the heart other than joy and peace. They are slight—"her heart sank a little," "it would be easier to undertake this effort"—but they are present. As yet, you do not see clearly in the discernment, but you are alive to the progression of the thoughts and the affective component of this discernment. You know that you need to give "much attention" to this as you and Kathy continue to meet.

Seventh Meeting

Kathy describes a difficult conversation with the parents of one student. She tells you that sometimes these days she finds it harder to be patient with such parents when she considers that they have so much—so much more than the poor—and yet complain about the school. Nonetheless, in general the past month has been blessed both in teaching and in prayer.

Kathy also says that if she were to teach in the Hispanic inner-city school, it would allow her to improve her Spanish, something she has always wanted to do. This would help her to work with the Hispanics in her parish and, on a more personal and spiritual note, help her read the great Carmelite spiritual masters—St. John of the Cross, St. Teresa of Avila—in the original. She has always loved Carmelite spirituality and has long desired to read these saints in Spanish in order to benefit more from them.

As you listen, you note further signs of affective trouble—she finds it "harder to be patient"—this time more obviously than in the preceding meeting. You remember also that Kathy did not speak of her heart sinking, of struggling to undertake a new effort, or of being impatient before the thoughts of the inner-city school arose. You begin to suspect that Ignatius's affective signs of the enemy may be present—that is, "If it [the course of the thoughts] weakens . . . or disquiets, or troubles the soul, taking away the peace, tranquility, and quiet, which it had before, it is a clear sign that it proceeds from the bad spirit."

You also note a further progression in the course of the thoughts. Kathy has spoken, for the first time, of Hispanic ministry in her parish. You wonder, too, whether there may not be something a little more self-centered—though focused on the spiritual life—in this new thought that teaching in Spanish would give her greater access to the Carmelite masters. You question now whether the more objective signs of the enemy may be appearing, as, for example, "something distracting." You do not have full clarity in the discernment, but you are aware that signs of the enemy may be emerging, and you will continue to give much attention to this as you and Kathy meet.

Eighth Meeting

Kathy expresses her irritation at her colleagues' unwillingness to help in the capital campaign and to accept limited classroom space during the renovations. She was sharp with one of her students and feels bad about this. She says, "I don't know what's happening to me. I just don't have the same peace. I get impatient with my students and at home more than I used to. I think that maybe the inner-city school is the answer. I even wonder sometimes whether it might be time for me to stop teaching. I've done it for many years. Maybe I've given what I can."

Kathy has now reached the "end" of which Ignatius speaks in Second Rules, 5: she feels that God is calling her to the inner-city school. She says, "I think that maybe the inner-city school is the answer." Now you find that signs of the enemy—affective and objective diminishment with respect to what Kathy had before the thought of the inner-city school arose—are evident. They are clear because you have helped Kathy give much attention to her spiritual experience, and you have done so as well. When you compare the peace and fruitful service that Kathy had before the thought of the inner-city school arose with her present condition, the "descent" (Second Rules, 6) is apparent.

You help Kathy see this by explaining her experience in light of Second Rules, 5. She perceives the truth of this and is relieved to understand what has happened to her in these months. She dismisses the thought of the inner-city school and renews her dedication to her service in her present school. Her peace and joy return. She is grateful to you for helping her in a difficult discernment.

As this scenario shows, when a person is tempted under the appearance of good and Ignatius's Second Rules are properly applied, no harm comes to the person. For a period and with no fault of her own or yours, Kathy pursues such a temptation. When you apply Second Rules, 5, the temptation is unmasked, Kathy rejects it, and pursues her present fruitful service.

Second Scenario

We will presume now that the first scenario does not happen and that, instead, your meetings with Kathy develop in a second and different way. As in the preceding scenario, Kathy has shared with you her prayer with Luke 4:18 and her thoughts about the inner-city school.

Second Meeting

This takes place just as the corresponding meeting in the first scenario. Kathy's teaching and prayer are alive and joyful, and the thought of the inner-city school repeats, always accompanied by a sense of God's love and closeness.

Third Meeting

This, too, occurs as in the first scenario: Kathy's joy persists, and the thought of the inner-city school returns with spiritual consolation. As in the first scenario, you help Kathy to be at peace and encourage her to continue in prayer and review.

Fourth Meeting

Kathy continues to be consoled in her prayer and work. The thought of the inner-city school remains, always with joy and a feeling of God's love.

Fifth Meeting

Kathy tells you that her life has become happier and her teaching more blessed. Her joy makes her a better teacher, and her students are responding to her in a new way. Her colleagues, too, relate to her with new warmth and gratitude. The thought of the inner-city school often returns and always with consolation.

You mark the persistence of Kathy's thoughts about the inner-city school and the consolation that accompanies them. You remain attentive to Kathy's experience in this regard.

Sixth Meeting

Kathy tells you that a review of her present high school's buildings has concluded that renovations are necessary for the school's future. A new capital campaign would have to be undertaken, and the teachers would be involved. They would also have to teach in reduced quarters during the year of renovations that would follow the campaign. Kathy has long seen the need for these improvements and knows that the school will serve the students better because of them. She is eager to help in the campaign, and her enthusiasm encourages other teachers to participate as well.

Kathy's prayer continues to be consoled. She tells you that the thought of the inner-city school returns from time to time and always with spiritual warmth.

You note that, as the discernment progresses, Kathy remains joyful and her teaching fruitful. In fact, you see this joy and fruitfulness increase. You perceive no sign of the enemy whether affectively or objectively. You begin to think that the signs of the good spirit are present: as the discernment unfolds, the process appears to be "all good, inclined to all good." You will continue to give much attention to this as the discernment develops further.

Seventh Meeting

When you meet, you sense in Kathy a peace, joy, and eagerness to serve. A week ago, tension had arisen with the parents of one student, and Kathy's patient listening, evident care for their son, and desire to meet his needs won the hearts of both parents and son. Kathy hopes that he may now progress in a new way. The principal thanked Kathy for handling a sensitive situation so well.

Kathy tells you she is increasingly convinced that God is calling her to the inner-city school where so many students have such need and so few resources. Her eyes are alive as she says this, and you see her joy reflected in her face. This meeting strengthens your sense of the good spirit at work in Kathy's attraction to the inner-city school.

Eighth Meeting

Kathy says, "We've been discerning for some time now whether God is calling me to the inner-city school. I have to tell you that I think God is calling me to this school. The more I consider it, the happier I become, and this has been consistent. I see the effects in my daily life, too, at home and at work. I'm glad that we have not hurried the discernment and have given the process time. It seems to me, though, that the discernment is clear. What do you think?"

In terms of Second Rules, 5, Kathy has reached the "end": "I think God is calling me to this [the inner-city] school." You find yourself agreeing with Kathy. No sign of the enemy's diminishment and descent has appeared in the months of discernment. On the contrary, the process appears to be "all good, inclined to all good," the sign of the good spirit. In fact, Kathy's joy and service even grow during this time. In light of Second Rules, 5, you confirm Kathy's discernment.

In the first scenario, Ignatius's Second Rules, 5, has helped you perceive the enemy's temptations under the appearance of good. The signs of the end, when the enemy's tactic is most clear, have supplied the guidance that directors need. But Ignatius does not stop here. It is not enough for him to detect and reject the enemy's "hidden deceits" by the signs of the end. A review of the "middle" that led to that end will strengthen Kathy to avoid such deceits in the future. Ignatius now turns to this review.

CHAPTER 6

Preparation for the Future

RULE 6

Ignatius writes,

> Sixth Rule. The sixth: when the enemy of human nature has been perceived and known by his serpent's tail and the bad end to which he induces, it profits the person who was tempted by him to look immediately at the course of the good thoughts that he brought and the beginning of them, and how little by little he procured to make him descend from the sweetness and spiritual gladness in which he was, till he brought him to his depraved intention; so that with such an experience known and noted he may guard himself in the future from his customary deceits.

In the eighth meeting of the first scenario given above, you and Kathy have resolved the discernment regarding the inner-city school. You have seen the signs of affective and objective diminishment that reveal the enemy's temptation under the appearance of good. This moment—your eighth meeting—is the time when Second Rules, 6 applies, that is, "when the enemy of human nature has been perceived and known by his serpent's tail and the bad end to which he induces."[27]

Kathy has discerned the enemy by the signs of the end (Second Rules, 5). When this occurs, Ignatius says, "it profits the person who was tempted by him, to look immediately at the course of the good thoughts that he brought." "Immediately": when the experience is still fresh, when she will comprehend it most insightfully and with the greatest spiritual benefit. Kathy, without delay, is to review "the course of the good thoughts that he brought," or, said more fully, "the beginning of them, and how little by little he procured to make him [her] descend from the sweetness and spiritual gladness in which he [she] was, till he brought him [her] to his depraved intention."

Kathy knows *that* the enemy brought her to his end through a little-by-little progression. She does not as yet see *how* the enemy did this, that is, by what subtle steps and through which of her spiritual vulnerabilities. The review that Ignatius proposes will help her perceive the hidden deceits of the enemy in the little-by-little of his temptation.

Ignatius indicates the purpose of this review: "So that with such an experience known and noted he [she] may guard himself [herself] in the future from his customary deceits." "Known and noted": seen clearly, understood, expressed in writing, verbalized, grasped more fully in conversation with the director.

The discerner does this "so that . . . he [she] may guard himself [herself] in the future from his customary deceits." "Customary": the enemy is likely to attempt similar temptations under the appearance of good, conformed (Second Rules, 4) to *this* specific person. In Kathy's case, the temptation under the appearance of good is conformed to one who loves the Lord deeply, who eagerly pursues spiritual growth, and who loves and serves her students with a generous heart and professional competence.[28] When Kathy reviews the little-by-little of the enemy, when she unmasks any "apparent reasons, subtleties, and persistent fallacies" (Second Rules, 1) in his hidden deceits, when she identifies the gradual unfolding of the course of thoughts, she will indeed guard herself "in the future from his customary deceits."

You and Kathy are meeting for the eighth time (first scenario). You have discerned the signs of the enemy, and Kathy now knows that God is not calling her to the inner-city school. You have discussed this together, the discernment is clear, and Kathy is at peace. In view of Second Rules, 6, however, you are not done!

Now is the time for Second Rules, 6. You explain to Kathy what she is to review—the little-by-little progression of the enemy's temptation in the time of discernment; the small, subtle steps by which she, through no fault of her own (or yours), was brought to a diminishment of peace and generosity. You encourage her to do this soon—today, if possible—but in any case, without delay. You suggest that she write in her journal what emerges and that you discuss this together in your next meeting. Kathy grasps the value of this review and willingly agrees.

That evening, when the children are settled, Kathy opens her journal. Slowly and attentively she reads what she has written since the thought of the inner-city school arose. Now she perceives her gradual loss of peace. Now, too, she notices the course of thoughts that began with one inner-city school and led to further considerations and to another school. Kathy describes all this in her journal.

In your next meeting, she shares with you what she has written. You listen and with opportune questions help her understand her experience more fully. You both know that if the enemy attempts again to deceive Kathy through spiritual consolation and good and holy thoughts, she will be ready in a new way. Because her present experience is "known and noted," she will likely guard herself in the future from the enemy's customary deceits. You have rendered her a great service by proposing the review of Second Rules, 6.

IF WE RETURN to the paradigm of beginning-middle-end, one question remains. Ignatius has equipped directors and directees to discern by the signs of the end (Second Rules, 5). He has also taught us to identify the enemy in the middle (Second Rules, 6). What of the *beginning*? In this beginning, both spirits may bring consolation with preceding cause and good and holy thoughts of some new choice. Is it possible to discern the good spirit and the enemy in the very beginning? Could Kathy, for example, with the help of her director, discern which spirit is at work that day when she experiences consolation while praying with Luke 4:18 and when the thought of the inner-city school first arises?

Ignatius addresses this question in Second Rules, 7. If discernment in the beginning is possible, directors and directees will be greatly helped: the middle and end will never take place. If, however, such discernment is possible, it will be highly refined discernment precisely because the signs of the middle and end are not yet present. Discernment of the beginning will require discernment between the good spirit and the enemy when the enemy most successfully imitates the good spirit—that is, in the beginning of his deceptive spiritual consolation and the good and holy thoughts that accompany it.

CHAPTER 7

A Refined Discernment

RULE 7

Ignatius writes,

> Seventh Rule. The seventh: in those who proceed from good to better, the good angel touches such a soul sweetly, lightly and gently, as a drop of water that enters a sponge; and the bad touches it sharply and with noise and disquiet, as when the drop of water falls on a stone; and in those who proceed from bad to worse the above-said spirits touch in a contrary way; the cause of which is that the disposition of the soul is contrary or similar to the said angels; for when it is contrary, they enter with clamor and sensible disturbances, perceptibly; and when it is similar, they enter with silence, as in their own house through an open door.

The discernment of the seventh rule is discernment by the *initial affective resonance* of movements given by the good spirit or the enemy. If a person is moving "from good to better" (toward God and his will), the initial affective resonance of a movement by the good spirit will be sweet, light, and gentle, like a drop of water entering a sponge or persons entering their own house through an open door. The initial affective resonance will be sweet and gentle because the work of the good spirit and the person's movement toward God are in harmony.

In this same person moving toward God, the initial affective resonance of a movement of the enemy will be sharp, noisy, and disquieting, like a drop of water falling on a stone or persons entering a house that is not their own. The initial affective resonance will be sharp and disquieting because the work of the enemy and the person's movement toward God are not in harmony.

In a person who is moving "from bad to worse" (away from God and his will), this reverses: now the initial affective resonance of the good spirit will be sharp and disquieting and that of the enemy will be sweet and gentle. The reason is the same: the person's disposition (in this case, moving away from God) is not in harmony with the good spirit and is in harmony with the enemy.

How SHALL WE UNDERSTAND Second Rules, 7? Who are these persons moving from good to better or from bad to worse? Whom does Ignatius have in mind in Second Rules, 7?[29]

The commentators respond differently to this question. With varying nuances, they propose two interpretations. A first focuses primarily on the *text* of Second Rules, 7. In this interpretation, Ignatius supplies a universal criterion for discernment in any situation: if a person is moving toward God, the initial affective resonance of a movement of the good spirit will be sweet and gentle; that of the enemy, sharp and disquieting.

This reverses when a person heads away from God. For example, a person loves the Lord and has progressed spiritually. More recently, however, this person has grown somewhat tepid. The person is now "proceeding from bad to worse," and the two spirits will "touch" and "enter" in the manner Ignatius describes.

A second interpretation emphasizes more the *context* of Second Rules, 7. In this understanding, the persons moving "from good to better" and those moving "from bad to worse" are identified through the context of the Second Rules as a whole and of Second Rules, 7, as the *seventh* of these rules.[30]

In his Second Rules, Ignatius presumes the generous, dedicated persons of the second spiritual situation whom the enemy may tempt under the appearance of good—persons like Kathy (*SpirEx*, 10, 328). This is the context of his Second Rules.

More specifically, Second Rules, 7, follows upon Second Rules, 3–6. As these earlier rules indicate, the enemy brings these persons spiritual consolation with preceding cause accompanied by good and holy thoughts—but not thoughts that God wills for them. Thus, Kathy experiences spiritual consolation with preceding cause as she prays with Luke 4:18, in the course of which thoughts of teaching in the inner-city school arise. In Second Rules, 3–6, Ignatius tells us that such consolation and such thoughts may be of the enemy tempting under the appearance of good.

In Second Rules, 3, he affirms that both the good spirit and the enemy can give consolation with preceding cause. Then, in Second Rules, 4, he describes the three moments of the enemy's tactic when he does so: the beginning (when this consolation and these thoughts first arise), middle (the "little-by-little" descent as the course of the thoughts unfolds), and end (the person, if not discerning, is deceived and chooses the good and holy thing that God does not want). In Second Rules, 5, Ignatius helps us discern this tactic through objective and affective signs of descent, signs most evident in the end. Finally, in Second Rules, 6, he calls us to review the gradual descent of the middle and so learn from this for the future.

In view of this context—generally: the second set of rules, persons in the second spiritual situation, the enemy tempting under the appearance of good through consolation with preceding cause and good and holy thoughts; and specifically: the *seventh* rule of this set, following on Second Rules, 5, which helps us discern by the *end*, and Second Rules, 6, which helps us discern the *middle*—Second Rules, 7 would appear to focus on this same tactic of the enemy in its *beginning* and offer help to discern even then.

In the preceding rules, Ignatius focused on the "course of the thoughts" and what happened in the person as this unfolded. Obviously that criterion will not serve in the beginning since the course of the thoughts has not yet developed. Ignatius, therefore, presents a different criterion. He asks, "With what *initial affective resonance* did the good and holy thoughts first arise? Did they arise sweetly and gently or sharply and with disquiet?" This initial affective resonance, Ignatius affirms, offers a first indication as to whether these thoughts are of the good spirit or the enemy. In what follows, I will apply this interpretation of Second Rules, 7.[31]

LET US RETURN now to your initial meeting with Kathy (prologue) and examine it in light of Second Rules, 7. Five years ago, with your accompaniment, Kathy entered into discernment regarding the principal's request that she teach in the upscale high school and so contribute to its renewal. Her discernment was serious and well made. She concluded that God was calling her to the upscale high school, and you, hearing what she shared during this process, confirmed her decision.

Kathy has now taught in that school for five years. She has put her professional ability and her heart into serving her students. Kathy's teaching and presence, as the principal had foreseen, have blessed the school and contributed effectively to its growth toward viability. Her own spiritual life has deepened over these years. In Ignatius's terms, Kathy appears to be "proceeding from good to better"—that is, serving where God wants her to serve and doing so with fruit for her students, the school, and personally.

To illustrate Second Rules, 7, we will explore two scenarios of Kathy's meetings with you after she prays with Luke 4:18.

First Scenario

You meet, and Kathy tells you of her visit to the inner-city school three weeks earlier. Then she describes her experience of praying with Luke 4:18 a week after that visit.

She says, "I was praying with the day's Gospel as usual. The text was Luke 4:14–21, about Jesus's words in the synagogue at Nazareth. Verse 18, 'The Spirit of the Lord is upon me, because he has anointed me to preach good news to the poor,' especially spoke to my heart. I could see Jesus in the synagogue, standing, with the scroll of Isaiah in his hands, and reading the prophecy about his own mission. I saw the love in his eyes, his desire to serve the poor, to bring them good news, to free them from suffering, and to give them the joy of salvation. I was deeply, deeply struck by his love for the poor, that they were the first ones he mentioned when he described his mission."

As Kathy says this, you see that she is greatly moved. You listen with attention and reverence.

Kathy continues, "The prayer was warm and uplifting. I felt God's love and closeness. I felt the love in Jesus as he pronounced these words. They spoke to my heart and gave me joy. Then I thought of the inner-city school, of its poverty, of the difficult lives of the students, and of the need for qualified teachers there. I wondered, 'Lord, are you calling me to teach in that school? Is that what you are saying to me? Is that how you want me to love the poor? To love them as you love them? Is that how I can best serve you and your people?' The thought gave me joy and seemed, somehow, to bring me even closer to Jesus."

Kathy adds, "The thought of the inner-city school and this joy have returned from time to time since that day." Then she asks you, "Is this God's way of revealing a call to the inner-city school? Does this mean that God is asking me to teach there?"

You are aware that Kathy is a person in the second spiritual situation. You note that she has received spiritual consolation with preceding cause and that a good and holy thought has arisen with it: the thought of sharing more fully in Jesus's love for the poor by teaching in the inner-city school. You know that this consolation and this thought could be of the good spirit and an indication of where God is leading her. You also know that this consolation and thought might be of the enemy tempting Kathy under the appearance of good.

Can Second Rules, 7, help you respond to Kathy? In her present role as teacher, she appears to be a person "proceeding from good to better" in love and service of God. Does the new thought, when it first arises, enter her heart "sweetly, lightly, and gently," like a drop of water entering a sponge? Or when it first arises, does it enter "sharply and with noise and disquiet," like a drop of water falling on a stone? With what initial affective resonance does this thought arise?

In recounting the moment when the thought arises, Kathy does not mention even the slightest sense of trouble, anxiety, or heaviness of heart. With Second Rules, 7, in mind, you gently ask Kathy to describe that moment as best she can. She does so, and you help her with relevant questions. You listen attentively as she speaks about that moment, and you hear no trace of sharpness, noise, or disquiet; the thought appears to have arisen like a drop of water entering a sponge. You note that this could be a first sign of the good spirit, and you will keep this in mind in the process of discernment that will follow. That process remains necessary, but as it progresses, you will remember Kathy's description of this beginning and the absence of anything sharp or disquieting in it.

Second Scenario

All is the same as in the first scenario until Kathy describes her prayer further.

Kathy continues, "The prayer was warm and uplifting. I felt God's love and closeness. I felt the love in Jesus as he pronounced these words. They spoke to my heart and gave me joy. Then I thought of the inner-city school, of its poverty, of the difficult lives of the students, and of the need for qualified teachers there. I wondered, 'Lord, are you calling me to teach in that school? Is that what you are saying to me? Is that how you want me to love the poor? To love them as you love them? Is that how I can best serve you and your people?' I have to say that the thought was initially a little troubling, but it did give me joy and seemed, somehow, to bring me even closer to Jesus."

Kathy adds, "The thought of the inner-city school and this joy have returned from time to time since that day." Then she asks you, "Is this God's way of revealing a call to the inner-city school? Does this mean that God is asking me to teach there?"

As ABOVE, YOU ARE AWARE that Kathy is a person in the second spiritual situation. You note that she has received spiritual consolation with preceding cause and that a good and holy thought has arisen with it: the thought of sharing more fully in Jesus's love for the poor by teaching in the inner-city school. You know that this consolation and this thought could be of the good spirit and an indication of where God is leading her. You also know that this consolation and thought might be of the enemy tempting Kathy under the appearance of good.

In this second scenario, can Second Rules, 7, help you respond to Kathy? As said, she appears to be a person "proceeding from good to better" in love and service of God. Does the new thought, when it first arises, enter her heart "sweetly, lightly, and gently," like a drop of water entering a sponge? Or, when it first arises, does it enter "sharply and with noise and disquiet," like a drop of water falling on a stone? With what initial affective resonance does this thought arise?

You have listened attentively to Kathy's account of her prayer. You recognize that she has received spiritual consolation with preceding cause and that with it, a good and holy thought has arisen. This time, however, you note a slightly discordant touch when the thought first arises: "I have to say that the thought was initially a little troubling, but it did give me joy and seemed, somehow, to bring me even closer to Jesus." You recognize that this small initial sense of trouble might be a sign of the enemy—that is, that the thought has entered "sharply and with noise and disquiet," like a drop of water falling on a stone. You know that a process of discernment will be necessary, but you will remember this initial disquiet, aware that it might be a first sign of the enemy tempting under the appearance of good.

Kathy may not mention this initial trouble when she recounts her prayer with Luke 4:18. It may be submerged in her focus on the greater sense of joy as she prayed. Most likely she will not be aware of its significance. You, however, as her director and aware of Second Rules, 7, will invite her to describe that initial moment more fully. If she can, this troubling movement may emerge.

As mentioned, in both the first and the second scenario, you are unlikely to consider the discernment complete. You have noted a first indication that the good spirit (first scenario) or the enemy (second scenario) may be at work in the thought of the inner-city school, and this is valuable input toward discernment. You will accompany Kathy in the process of discernment to follow and watch as "the course of the thoughts" unfolds. You will "give much attention" as this course progresses, alert for signs of the one or the other spirit. You will do this with an open mind but also with a first surmise as to which spirit may be at work.

As is evident, discernment by Second Rules, 7, is highly refined. In all probability, most often you will not see clearly when directees share experiences like Kathy's. Again, there is no shame in this. Precisely because he knows this will often be so, Ignatius gives us rules for discernment by the end (Second Rules, 5) and the middle (Second Rules, 6). The presupposition in both rules is that discernment by the beginning was not sufficiently clear.

When the enemy has been discovered by the descent of the end, Ignatius says, "it profits the person who was tempted by him to look immediately at the course of the good thoughts that he brought, *and the beginning of them*, and how little by little he procured to make him descend from the sweetness and spiritual gladness in which he was" (Second Rules, 6). If you invite Kathy to make this review after the discernment is clear, she will grow in awareness of the enemy not only in the middle but also in the beginning. She will mature in discernment as Ignatius intends.

CHAPTER 8

The Time During and the Time After

RULE 8

In his final rule, Ignatius returns to the spiritual consolation without preceding cause discussed in Second Rules, 2. Here, however, he focuses on the time *immediately following* such consolation and highlights a pitfall to be avoided during it. Ignatius writes,

> Eighth Rule. The eighth: when the consolation is without cause, although there is no deception in it, since it is of God our Lord alone, as has been said, nevertheless the spiritual person to whom God gives such a consolation should, with much vigilance and attention, look at and distinguish the time itself of such an actual consolation from the time following, in which the soul remains warm and favored with the favor and remnants of the past consolation; for frequently, in this second time, through his own reasoning by associating and drawing consequences from ideas and judgments, or through the good spirit, or through the bad, he forms different proposals and opinions that are not given immediately by God our Lord, and therefore they must be very well examined before entire credit is given them or they are put into effect.

This rule, Ignatius tells us, applies in a specific circumstance: a person in the second spiritual situation has received spiritual consolation without preceding cause. This person—with your help—"should, with much vigilance and attention, look at and distinguish the time itself of such an actual consolation from the time following, in which the soul remains warm and favored with the favor and remnants of the past consolation."

Your directee, then, should carefully distinguish the *time itself* of the consolation without preceding cause from the *time immediately following*. This should be done "with much vigilance and attention": the vocabulary stresses the importance of this distinction.

In Kathy's experience (chapter 2, consolation without preceding cause as she walks in the woods), this means that she must carefully distinguish the *time itself* of the consolation without preceding cause ("I don't know how long this lasted: maybe ten minutes, maybe fifteen, maybe more") from the *time following* ("The joy of that experience is gentler now, but it has not left me").

Why is it important to distinguish these two times? Ignatius explains, "For frequently, in this second time, through his own reasoning by associating and drawing consequences from ideas and judgments, or through the good spirit, or through the bad, he forms different proposals and opinions that are not given immediately by God our Lord." From experience, Ignatius knows that often, in the warmth of the time following, the person will "form different proposals and opinions," adding in some way to what God gave during the time itself of the consolation without preceding cause. These proposals (views regarding things to be done) and opinions (ways of perceiving certain realities), he says, "must be very well examined before entire credit is given them or they are put into effect."

After consolation without preceding cause has been received, the person remains warmed by it. (Kathy: "The joy of that experience is gentler now, but it has not left me.") What was given *during* the consolation without preceding cause is surely of God and may be unhesitatingly followed. (Kathy: "And while this was happening, I knew that God is calling me to teach in the inner-city school. It was so clear that I couldn't doubt it.") This is so, Ignatius affirms, because "there is no deception *in it*, since it is of God our Lord alone."

The same guarantee does not apply to the *time following* the consolation without preceding cause. In this "second time," when the consolation without preceding cause is no longer present, the person "remains warm and favored with the favor and remnants of the past consolation." (Kathy: she remains joyful that evening and during the subsequent days.)

In this warm time following, Ignatius writes, "*different* proposals and opinions that are not given immediately by God our Lord" may arise. They may arise from the person's *own reasoning* about the grace given, or through the *good spirit*, or through the *bad spirit*.[32] In fact, Ignatius tells us, this frequently occurs. When it does, these different proposals and opinions "must be *very well examined* before entire credit is given them or they are put into effect."

What form might such "different proposals and opinions" take? With goodwill, but unaware that the guarantee of the time itself no longer holds, the person may add to, subtract from, or change in some way the "proposals and opinions" given by God during the consolation without preceding cause. To illustrate this, we will return to Kathy's meeting with you after her day of retreat (chapter 2) and develop it further.

When Kathy arrives, you note immediately that she is deeply moved. She tells you that last Saturday afternoon she went to a local retreat house. She goes there for a few hours when she can and loves the peace and quiet prayer the house affords her.

Once there, Kathy prayed for a time, and then in midafternoon, she went out walking. She enjoyed the silence, the freshness of the winter cold, the snow, and the trees that overhung the path. She walked, thinking of nothing in particular, simply absorbing her surroundings.

Kathy says, "Then something happened that I've never experienced before. I don't quite know how to describe it. One minute I was just walking through the woods, and then suddenly my heart was totally filled with a sense of God's love. It was overwhelming to feel so deeply, deeply loved. I was completely happy—the happiest I think I've ever been. God was close to me, loving me in a way I've never felt before. I don't know how long this lasted: maybe ten minutes, maybe fifteen, maybe more. I was so caught up in it, there was such sweetness and joy in it, that I could only receive it. And while this was happening, I knew that God is calling me to the inner-city school. It was so clear that I couldn't doubt it. The joy of that experience is gentler now but it has not left me."

She continues, "That gift of grace and the joy of it remained with me for some days after that experience. I was joyful, and I felt God's closeness, his love enveloping me. I wanted to respond fully to the Lord's call, to embrace this new step from the heart. I want that even now as I teach in my present school.

"When I visited the inner-city school, they asked if I would consider tutoring students on Saturdays. They urgently need such tutors. I think that this could be a good way to begin the transition. There might be other ways to get involved, and tutoring on Saturdays might open the door to them. I decided that I would speak with the principal of that school about this.

"I've thought, too, that the transition would be smoother if I begin, even now, to withdraw from various roles I've had these past years and start preparing others to assume them. I could also make the transition sooner if we change our family's plans for vacation this summer. I can talk with my husband about this."

Kathy looks at you and says, "I only want to say a complete yes to the Lord's call." She adds, "My friend Claire and I have often talked about serving the poor. I'm sure that if I share my plans with her, she'll be interested. I could invite her to join me in tutoring on Saturdays."

WITH SECOND RULES, 8, IN MIND, you are aware that these "proposals and opinions" arise in the time following Kathy's experience of consolation without preceding cause. Also with this rule in mind, you know that these thoughts and plans must be examined—Ignatius says "very well examined"—before Kathy puts them into effect. They may have arisen from Kathy's own reasoning, they may be inspired by the good spirit, or they may be of the enemy.

Ignatius's Second Rules, 8, does not say that these thoughts, because they arise in the time following, should be rejected. Through the person's reasoning guided by grace or through the work of the good spirit, these thoughts may express God's desire for the person. This rule says that they should be well examined before they are adopted. Through well-intentioned but flawed reasoning or through the influence of the enemy, they may lead the person away from God's desire and so cause harm. Because these thoughts do not have the guarantee of the time during, they should be well examined "before entire credit is given them or they are put into effect."

You explain Second Rules, 8, to Kathy, and she appreciates its wisdom. She will not act on these thoughts until, with your help, she has examined them well. You invite her to continue to pray and to note any further spiritual experience in this regard. Your counsel, your reassurance, and your accompaniment give peace to Kathy as she discerns these steps.

Conclusion

You have accompanied Kathy in her discernment regarding the inner-city school. In a first scenario, she, with your help, saw that God was not calling her to the inner-city school. This became clear as the course of her thoughts unfolded and signs of diminishment appeared (Second Rules, 5). The thought of the inner-city school was of the enemy tempting under the appearance of good.

In a second scenario, Kathy, with your help, saw that God was in fact calling her to the inner-city school. This became clear as the course of her thoughts unfolded and no signs of diminishment appeared. Kathy remained joyful and open to all good, even more than before this thought arose (again, Second Rules, 5).

In either scenario, Kathy benefited greatly from your help in applying Ignatius's Second Rules. Because you shared these rules with her, she knew that temptations under the appearance of good were possible. She understood that at this point in her spiritual journey, consolation and good and holy thoughts did not of themselves resolve a discernment, that the enemy might imitate the good spirit in an attempt to deceive, and that, therefore, such consolation and thoughts must be well discerned before acting upon them. Understanding this and with your accompaniment, she willingly entered a process of discernment.

Kathy prayed daily during the time of discernment. You explained the review of prayer, the examen, and journaling to her. She faithfully noted her spiritual experience and shared it when you met. In your first meetings, neither Kathy nor you saw clearly whether God wanted the inner-city school or not. You were at peace with this and helped Kathy also to be at peace. Both of you, in your respective roles, continued to be attentive. Gradually signs of diminishment or their absence clarified the discernment and it concluded.

Many fruits followed. Kathy could now direct her energies with joy toward the choice that God wills. If the thought of the inner-city school was a temptation under the appearance of good, because you have helped her apply Ignatius's Second Rules, Kathy suffered no spiritual harm. In addition, the many people affected by her discernment are spared any loss.

Having experienced Ignatius's Second Rules, Kathy has grown in discernment. As Ignatius intends (Second Rules, 6), she will discern similar temptations more readily in the future.

When her discernment concluded, Kathy was grateful to God. She was also deeply grateful to you for your guidance in a refined discernment.

You, too, were grateful to God who assisted you as you helped Kathy discern. You were grateful also to Ignatius, whose Second Rules proved indispensable in accompanying Kathy. Because you walked with Kathy in this discernment, you understand these Second Rules better. You know that what you learned will bless your future direction.

What if, having applied Ignatius's Second Rules in the manner described, questions regarding the discernment remain? With your help, Kathy has applied the rules but has not attained the clarity she needs. What then?

When this occurs, neither you nor Kathy is at fault. God, Ignatius says, is calling Kathy to discern according to a further mode.

In a first mode of discernment, God simply makes the discernment clear. In a second—to which Ignatius's Second Rules belong—God gives clarity through discernment of spirits—that is, through applying the First Rules (if the discernment involves spiritual consolation and desolation) or the Second Rules (if the discernment involves temptations under the appearance of good). When clarity has not been given through first- or second-mode discernment, God is calling the person to discern according to a third mode.[33]

In this third mode, a person discerns through reason enlightened by faith and aided by grace. The person prayerfully reviews the advantages and disadvantages for God's greater glory of both options. For Kathy, these options are the move to the inner-city school or remaining in the upscale school. The option that presents a preponderance of reasons for God's greater glory is shown to be God's will.[34]

How OFTEN IN SPIRITUAL DIRECTION will you need the Second Rules? Certainly less than the First Rules. But when you accompany a person in the second spiritual situation, Ignatius's Second Rules will be vital for discernment. If you have read this book, it is because you appreciate their importance.

As I have explored the Second Rules over the years, I have come to marvel at Ignatius's achievement. Guided by the Spirit, he addressed the most refined discernment a person may face and shaped a concise and practical path to clarity: eight rules, 677 words, that guide those engaged in such discernment.

May this book give directors greater confidence and proficiency in applying these eight rules. And may their wisdom bless both director and directee, and their fruit, God's people.

APPENDIX

Deceptions through Energy: An Ignatian Survey

Ignatius's Second Rules are concerned with one refined deception through energy: the enemy tempts a person in the second spiritual situation under the appearance of good, bringing consolation with good and holy thoughts.[35] In his Spiritual Exercises, Ignatius discusses a broader array of deceptions through energy. I will review them here. Clarity regarding them will help identify the precise deception through energy contemplated by the Second Rules.

I will present each through an example and then describe it in the light of Ignatius's teaching.[36] In each case, again following Ignatius, I will supply the appropriate remedy for the deception involved.

Example 1: John

> John is a young, single professional in his late twenties. Since college, he has abandoned the sacraments and all involvement in the Church. Influenced by others, he adopted, at first hesitantly and then with increasing willingness, a life of self-indulgence and promiscuity. He also engages in seriously dishonest dealings in his work. His friends now invite him to spend a week in the Caribbean. John knows that this will be a week without moral restraint. He is excited by the possibility and makes the necessary plans with enthusiasm.

This is clearly a deception through energy—John is "excited" and makes his plans "with enthusiasm"—but equally clearly, neither the person nor the deception match Ignatius's criteria for the Second Rules. John's experience is that described in First Rules, 1: "In persons who are going from mortal sin to mortal sin, the enemy is ordinarily accustomed to propose apparent pleasures to them, leading them to imagine sensual delights and pleasures in order to hold them more and make them grow in their vices and sins."

This spiritual experience is the furthest removed from that of the person in the second spiritual situation and the Second Rules. The remedy is to welcome the stinging and biting action of the good spirit (First Rules, 1, second part) and so turn from sin and toward God.

Example 2: Martha

> Martha is making her first directed retreat. The initial days have been a time of discouragement: prayer has been difficult, God has seemed distant, and on several occasions she has nearly abandoned the retreat. But today all that has changed. Prayer has been warm and joyful, the scriptural texts have come alive, and God has felt close. Now Martha is certain that her problems are over, that her spiritual struggles are finished, that heaviness of heart will no longer burden her spiritual life. She dedicates herself with great energy to prayer as the day continues.

Martha experiences genuine spiritual consolation. As she prays, she is filled with joy and God feels close. She appears unaware, however, of the pitfall addressed in First Rules, 10: "Let the one who is in consolation think how he will conduct himself in the desolation that will come after, taking new strength for that time." If Martha, in her time of spiritual consolation, prepares for the eventual return of spiritual desolation, that desolation is less likely to harm her. The danger here is from naivete and its consequences when spiritual desolation returns. The need is wise provision for future desolation.

Example 3: Clare

> Clare began daily prayer with Scripture three months ago. Each morning she dedicates half an hour to this prayer. At first, though she was faithful, she found the prayer dry and difficult. In recent

> weeks, however, she has felt God's closeness and his love in her daily prayer. This awareness of God's love gives joy to her heart throughout the occupations of the day. She is filled with satisfaction that she has achieved so rich an ability to pray and is pleased to see herself progressing so surely in her spiritual life.

Clare's experience, too, is authentic spiritual consolation. She perceives this and "is filled with satisfaction that she has achieved so rich an ability to pray" and is "pleased to see herself progressing so surely in her spiritual life." In First Rules, 11, Ignatius writes, "Let one who is consoled seek to humble himself and lower himself as much as he can, thinking of how little he is capable in the time of desolation without such grace or consolation" (see also First Rules, 9, third cause). The danger here is self-satisfaction. Clare, almost unconsciously, ascribes the gift she has received to her own abilities. Her need, therefore, is for a wise humility. Such humility will bless Clare as her journey of prayer continues.

Both Martha and Clare need Ignatius's help in regard to their spiritual consolation. As is evident, however, we are far from the second spiritual situation and the enemy's temptations under the appearance of good. Martha and Clare appear to be persons in the first spiritual situation: Martha is making her first directed retreat and Clare began prayer with Scripture three months earlier. Both responses to spiritual consolation, the one naïve and the other self-satisfied, are addressed in Ignatius's First Rules.

Example 4: Mark

> Mark is a university student who is easily moved by enthusiasm. Most often, however, his enthusiasm does not endure. Recently a friend invited him to a retreat. Mark was struggling with loneliness at the time and willingly accepted the invitation. He was deeply struck by the sense of community and fraternal love he found among the participants. Now, filled with joy in the Lord, Mark is certain that he has at last found his way. He desires to embrace this

> new life fully, and he decides to become a priest. He plans to interrupt his studies and apply for admission to the local seminary. Mark enthusiastically shares his decision with the university chaplain.

This, too, is an experience of spiritual consolation. Mark is "filled with joy in the Lord." In *Spiritual Exercises*, annotation 14, Ignatius writes, "If the one who gives the Exercises sees that the one receiving them is going on in consolation and with much fervor, he should warn him not to make any inconsiderate and hasty promise or vow; and the more light of character he knows him to be, the more he should warn and admonish him."

Mark's decision does indeed have something "inconsiderate and hasty" about it, and Ignatius's annotation 14 fully applies to him. The remedy is also given in this annotation: "He [the one giving the Spiritual Exercises or the spiritual director in daily life] must carefully consider the character and strength of the person and how much help or hindrance he will find in carrying out the thing he wishes to promise."

The distance here from the second spiritual situation is evident.

Example 5: Andrew

> Andrew is a married man in his thirties who, after years away from the Church, six months ago embraced his faith with new commitment and energy. Aware of this, and knowing his business skills, his pastor asked Andrew to serve on the parish financial council. Andrew was happy to accept. Now he delights in exercising his ability to handle financial matters effectively. Gradually he increases his involvement in the financial council. This additional activity, together with his responsibilities to family and work, strains his energies.

Once more, we witness a potential pitfall through energy. Further, it occurs through involvement in "sacred" things—the life of the parish.

Questions arise, however, regarding whether this experience pertains to the Second Rules. Andrew—a man who "after years away from the

Church, six months ago embraced his faith with new commitment and energy"—is more a beginner than the mature spiritual person of the second spiritual situation.

In addition, though his service is to the parish, his consolation appears to be more nonspiritual (psychological) than spiritual: "He delights in exercising his ability to handle financial matters effectively." Nothing in the vocabulary indicates a specifically spiritual consolation.

If Andrew continues to expand his role, his current strain will increase and harmful consequences will follow. This will be evident to any attentive observer. The fact that the setting is the Church does not change the issue: Andrew enjoys exercising his financial abilities and is tending, at present, to pursue this task to the detriment of his other commitments and ultimately to his own well-being.

In this and similar cases, Ignatius's Second Rules are not needed. What *is* needed is the virtue of prudence by which we choose wisely the means to an end. The end in this case is contribution to the financial well-being of the parish so that it may serve its members well. The prudent means will be an involvement that allows Andrew to contribute to this goal compatibly with his other responsibilities and his health.

The difference between these cases and that of Kathy is clear. By contrast with these others, Kathy is very much the spiritually mature person of the second spiritual situation. She experiences spiritual consolation as she prays with Luke 4:18. As she does, the thought of the inner-city school arises as a step toward deeper communion with Jesus and greater service to the poor.

Ignatius tells us that in such persons, such consolations and thoughts may be either of the good spirit or the enemy tempting under the appearance of good. How will Kathy know? How will she discern in a matter of such importance for her and for those affected by her discernment?

Obviously the guidance provided for the earlier cases will not help Kathy and her director. Here, only Ignatius's Second Rules will assist Kathy. Ignatius provides them precisely for such situations.

Notes

1. These are found respectively in Spiritual Exercises, para. 313–327 (First Rules) and para. 328–336 (Second Rules). Ignatius's own titles to these rules refer to the corresponding weeks in the Spiritual Exercises: "These rules are more proper for the first week" (First Rules, 313), and "They help more for the second week" (Second Rules, 328). In adopting "First Rules" and "Second Rules," I envisage the application of these rules outside of the Spiritual Exercises as well. Throughout this book, all translations of texts from the Spiritual Exercises are the author's.

2. I discuss these rules in detail in the following: *The Discernment of Spirits: An Ignatian Guide for Everyday Living* (New York: Crossroad, 2005); *Setting Captives Free: Personal Reflections on Ignatian Discernment of Spirits* (New York: Crossroad, 2018); *Discernment of Spirits in Marriage: Ignatian Wisdom for Husbands and Wives* (Manchester, NH: Sophia Institute Press, 2020); *The Discerning Priest: Ignatian Wisdom for Daily Life in Priesthood* (Omaha, NE: IPF Publications, 2021).

3. Timothy M. Gallagher, OMV, *Spiritual Consolation: An Ignatian Guide for the Greater Discernment of Spirits* (New York: Crossroad, 2007). See also the series on YouTube: https://www.youtube.com/watch?v=hpUktn0ivek.

4. See Timothy M. Gallagher, OMV, "The Discernment of Spirits: When Do the Second Week Rules Apply?" *The Way* 47, nos. 1–2 (January/April 2008): 126–42. See also, Gallagher, *Spiritual Consolation*, 135–72. In the endnotes to the book, I explore the various issues of interpretation.

5. I wish to acknowledge my debt to two authors whose excellent commentaries on the First and Second Rules have helped me greatly: Jules Toner, SJ, *A Commentary on Saint Ignatius' Rules for the Discernment of Spirits: A Guide to the Principles and Practice* (St. Louis: Institute of Jesuit Sources, 1982); and Daniel Gil, SJ, *Discernimiento según San Ignacio: Exposición y comentario practico de las dos series de reglas de discernimiento de espíritus contenidas en el libro de los Ejercicios Espirituales de San Ignacio de Loyola (EE 313–336)* (Rome: Centrum Ignatianum Spiritualitatis, 1983). To both, I am deeply grateful.

6. All biblical texts, unless otherwise noted, are from RSVCE.

7. Ignatius also speaks of spiritual consolation and spiritual desolation in annotations 6 and 7: If the retreatant does not experience these, the one who gives the retreat should explore with him his manner of living the retreat (6); if the retreatant experiences spiritual desolation and temptations, the one who gives the retreat should be gentle with him and encouraging (7).

8. See, for example: *SpirEx*, 13, 317, 320.

9. Gil, *Discernimiento según San Ignacio*, 271. Author's translation.

10. How often will directors encounter such persons? They are very likely to meet persons in the second spiritual situation. Michael Kyne, SJ, however, adds a caveat against assuming too quickly that a directee is, in fact, in this spiritual situation: "It is a fact of my experience, brief though that may be, that by far the greater number of problems concerning Christian living, even for religious and priests, occur on a level of discernment which is not related to a such a settled aim of a generous service of God. The discernment is, so often, no more than that exercised by beginners in the Christian life—according to the rules set out in the first week of the Exercises." *The Way Supplement* 6 (1968): 23. See Gallagher, *Spiritual Consolation*, 139n17.

11. See Gil, *Discernimiento*, 277, and Gallagher, *Spiritual Consolation*, 14–29.

12. In Kathy's consistent attraction to the inner-city school in time of spiritual consolation, directors will note the possibility of a second-mode discernment (*SpirEx*, 176). Wisely, directors will allow the process to continue until, should God so choose, "sufficient clarity and understanding" (*SpirEx*, 176) for discernment is given. For second-mode discernment, see Timothy Gallagher, OMV, *A Handbook for Spiritual Directors: An Ignatian Guide for Accompanying Discernment of God's Will* (New York: Crossroad, 2017), 67–109. See also, Gallagher, *Discerning the Will of God: An Ignatian Guide to Christian Decision Making* (New York: Crossroad, 2009), 83–101.

13. For an in-depth discussion of Second Rules, 2, and the consolation without preceding cause it describes, see Gallagher, *Spiritual Consolation*, 40–56, with the notes to this chapter. Directors will note that Kathy, together with spiritual consolation without preceding cause, also receives a first-mode discernment. For first-mode discernment, see Gallagher, *A Handbook for Spiritual Directors*, 53–66, and *Discerning the Will of God*, 69–82.

14. Ruth Burrows, OCD, *Before the Living God* (Cornwall: Hidden Spring, 2008), 72–73.

15. On spiritual and nonspiritual consolation, see Gallagher, *Discernment of Spirits*, 48–51.

16. Account of a Carmelite, aged fifty, thirty years in religious life. In Bernard Bro, OP, *Contemplative Nuns Speak* (Baltimore and Dublin: Helicon Press, 1964), 43–44.

17. See Gallagher, *Spiritual Consolation*, 56 and 150n31.

18. Ignatius focuses on the time *immediately* preceding the abundant experience of spiritual consolation. In Kathy's case, she is walking through the woods, thinking of nothing in particular, simply absorbing her surroundings. In this time, Kathy is not praying or focusing her mind and heart on any spiritual object.

19. See Gallagher, *Spiritual Consolation*, 150n29.

20. Gil, *Discernimiento según San Ignacio*, 301. See Gallagher, *Spiritual Consolation*, 150n31.

21. See, however, the conclusion of this book and its discussion of when God may not give clarity through the application of the Second Rules and discerners may need Ignatius's third mode of discernment.

22. In the first spiritual situation, his deceits are "manifest" (First Rules, 13).

23. Timothy Gallagher, OMV, *The Examen Prayer: Ignatian Wisdom for Our Lives Today* (New York: Crossroad, 2006), and the podcast series *The Daily Examen* on discerninghearts.com and the Discerning Hearts app.

24. Jules Toner, SJ, *A Commentary on Saint Ignatius' Rules for the Discernment of Spirits: A Guide to the Principles and Practice* (St. Louis: Institute of Jesuit Sources, 1982), 230.

25. "Ignatius is talking about a process, a series of thoughts and affections in which there is some continuity from the starting point to the termination. . . . There may be minutes, hours, even days, between the steps of the process. Nevertheless, there is continuity and process if each new step takes up from the earlier steps, builds on them, and develops them toward the goal that gives them unity and purpose. Thus, a person may put aside a course of thoughts from weariness or because of other calls on his or her attention, only to take it up again later. Or a passing thought may come now, another at another time, and so on, but with all of them converging and building up an attitude of mind and heart. Or a thought comes and goes, and hours or days later comes back and by association leads to a different one, and so on until the person reaches the one the tempter intends. He or she may not even be aware that there is continuity, a process, until after reflection on the whole experience." Toner, *Commentary*, 225.

26. The discernment will be clear if God is, in fact, calling the person to discern according to the Second Rules. For a discussion of this issue, see the conclusion to this book.

27. "Serpent's tail and the bad end": two ways of saying the same—one metaphorical, the other literal.

28. "In the first spiritual situation, the enemy tempted spiritually progressing persons through their *weak* point (First Rules, 14); in the second spiritual situation, the enemy attempts to deceive generously dedicated persons through their *strong* point." Gallagher, *Spiritual Consolation*, 154n5.

29. See Gallagher, *Spiritual Consolation*, 161–63n1, where I discuss this question in detail and to which I refer the reader for the commentators and their works.

30. "Ignatius speaks of these dedicated persons as proceeding 'from good to better' or 'from bad to worse.' When the good and holy thoughts they are pursuing correspond to God's true desire for them—when such thoughts are 'all good' and 'inclined to all good' (*Second Rules*, 5)—then these persons are proceeding *from good to better*. And

when, even though without awareness of the fact and so without moral culpability, these persons are pursuing deceptive good and holy thoughts of the enemy which do not correspond to God's true desire for them—and which lead, therefore, to something objectively or subjectively less good than what they had proposed before (*Second Rules*, 5)—they are, in this sense, proceeding *from bad to worse*." Gallagher, *Spiritual Consolation*, 104.

31. I do so because I find this interpretation the most compelling. In it we attend both to the text, the words Ignatius uses, and to the context of Second Rules, 7.

32. Ignatius writes to Teresa Rejadell: "But we can frequently be deceived, however, because after such consolation or inspiration, when the soul is still abiding in its joy, the enemy tries under the impetus of this joy to make us innocently add to what we have received from God our Lord. His only purpose is to disturb and confuse us in everything. At other times he makes us lessen the import of the message we have received and confronts us with obstacles and difficulties, so as to prevent us from carrying out completely what had been made known to us. Right here there is more need of attention than anywhere else. . . . The enemy thus tries to magnify or diminish the communication received." Letter of June 18, 1536, in William Young, SJ, trans., *Letters of St. Ignatius of Loyola* (Chicago: Loyola University Press, 1959), 22–23.

33. *SpirEx*, 177–188.

34. For an in-depth treatment of these three modes, see the two books cited above: Timothy Gallagher, OMV, *A Handbook for Spiritual Directors: An Ignatian Guide for Accompanying Discernment of God's Will* and *Discerning the Will of God: An Ignatian Guide to Christian Decision Making*. Should third-mode discernment always be employed even when discernment by the second mode appears to be clear? The commentators are divided on this question. See Gallagher, *A Handbook for Spiritual Directors*, 145–47. The more important the discernment, the more likely directors will be to counsel third-mode discernment in addition to the second mode.

35. His First Rules deal with a temptation through a deficit of energy: the discouragement of spiritual desolation with its accompanying temptations.

36. I cite these with adaptation from Timothy Gallagher, OMV, "The Discernment of Spirits: When Do the Second Week Rules Apply?" *The Way* 47, nos. 1–2 (January–April 2008): 132–37. Used with permission.

Resources

Books

Timothy M. Gallagher, OMV, *Spiritual Consolation: An Ignatian Guide for the Greater Discernment of Spirits*. New York: Crossroad, 2007.

Timothy M. Gallagher, OMV, *The More Discerning Priest: Mature Discernment in Diocesan Priesthood*. Omaha, NE: IPF Publications, 2023.

Timothy M. Gallagher, OMV, *A Handbook for Spiritual Directors: An Ignatian Guide for Accompanying Discernment of God's Will*. New York: Crossroad, 2017.

Article

Timothy M. Gallagher, OMV, "The Discernment of Spirits: When Do the Second Week Rules Apply?" *The Way* 47, nos. 1–2 (Jan/April 2008): 126–42.

Podcasts

Timothy M. Gallagher, OMV, "Second Week Rules for Greater Discernment," 14 episodes, Discerning Hearts, https://www.discerninghearts.com/catholic-podcasts/fr-timothy-gallagher-the-second-week-rules-for-the-discernment-of-spirits-discerning-hearts-podcasts/ and Discerning Hearts app.

YouTube

Timothy M. Gallagher, OMV, "Second Week Rules for Greater Discernment," 14 episodes, https://www.youtube.com/watch?v=hpUktn0ivek.

For all of Fr. Gallagher's materials, see: frtimothygallagher.org.

About the Author

Timothy M. Gallagher was ordained to the priesthood in 1979 as a member of the Congregation of the Oblates of the Virgin Mary. In 1983, he obtained his doctorate from The Pontifical Gregorian University, and became a spiritual director and retreat leader. He has taught at St. John's Seminary, Brighton, and Our Lady of Grace Seminary Residence, Boston, both in Massachusetts. In 2015, Father Gallagher accepted the St. Ignatius Chair for Spiritual Formation at St. John Vianney Theological Seminary in Denver. He has written over twenty books on spiritual themes, published articles in Catholic periodicals, appears frequently on Catholic television, and records many podcasts, radio interviews, series on YouTube, and virtual events used throughout the English-speaking Catholic world.

www.ingramcontent.com/pod-product-compliance
Lightning Source LLC
LaVergne TN
LVHW091204080426
835509LV00006B/831
9780824589035